W9-BKL-169

Youth
Ministry
Handbook

Youth Ministry Handbook

Edward A. Trimmer

ABINGDON PRESS
Nashville

YOUTH MINISTRY HANDBOOK

Copyright © 1994 by Abingdon Press

This book is printed on recycled, acid-free paper.

Library of Congress Cataloging-in-Publication Data

Trimmer, Edward A.
    Youth ministry handbook / Edward A. Trimmer.
      p. cm.— (Essentials for Christian youth)
    ISBN 0-687-01034-9 (pbk. : alk. paper)
    1. Church work with youth. 2. Youth—Religious life. I. Title.
II.Series.
BV4447.T   IN PROCESS   94-28848
259'.23—dc20   CIP

98 99 00 01 02 03 — 10 9 8 7 6 5

MANUFACTURED IN THE UNITED STATES OF AMERICA

To the churches that nurtured and educated me about the Christian life while allowing me to be in ministry with them:

Verona United Methodist Church, Verona, New Jersey
Burgess Avenue United Methodist Church, Columbus, Ohio
Belle-Vista Simpson United Methodist Church, Clifton,
New Jersey
Oakdale United Methodist Church, Grand Rapids,
Michigan
Trinity United Methodist Church, Grand Rapids, Michigan
St. Pauls United Methodist Church, Kentwood, Michigan
South Wyoming United Methodist Church, Wyoming,
Michigan
First United Methodist Church, Decatur, Georgia
First United Methodist Church, Greensboro, Georgia
Covenant Presbyterian Church, Upper Arlington, Ohio
Hillside Presbyterian Church, Decatur, Georgia

THANKS!

and to my wife,
Peggy Sue,

God bless!

CONTENTS

89010

Is This Handbook
for You?

A Quick Health Checklist For Youth Ministry

- Are the youth events open to members of the church only?
- Does your church struggle with what to do with high school graduates who want to be a part of the youth group?
- Is youth fellowship what your church thinks of as youth ministry?
- Is your youth ministry just programmatic in nature?
- Does your youth ministry focus basically on youth?
- Does your church ask for adult volunteers for youth ministry from the pulpit?
- Are parents of teenagers always understood as the leaders of the youth ministry?
- Has your church made a decision to "concentrate" on the younger youth?
- Are youth expected to be on certain church committees but are never elected or, if elected, never participate?
- Does your congregation always expect the youth to lead certain events, such as an Easter sunrise service?

- Do the parents talk about youth ministry as a way to keep the youth busy or off the streets or out of trouble?
- Do members of your congregation think the youth ministry is too ambitious or requires too much of a commitment by youth?
- Does your church simply hire a youth pastor and turn everything over to him or her?
- Are the numbers of youth at Sunday school or youth group declining each year?
- Is there a budget squeeze at your church, resulting in a shrinking budget for youth?
- Do you serve some kind of meal at every youth group meeting?
- Do youth always get mailings from the church addressed to their parents?
- Do the adults at the church wonder what the names of the youth are?
- Do all the mailings to the church about youth ministry end up on the pastor's desk or in the trash can?
- Has your church's youth ministry had a succession of adults associated with the program over the past five years?

If the answers to many of these questions are yes, then the youth ministry at your church may be in trouble. If you are interested in thinking about the youth ministry of your church in a new and dynamic way, or if you wonder why answering yes to these questions may mean that the youth ministry of your congregation is in trouble, this handbook is for you.

CHAPTER 1

Rethinking
Youth Ministry

Jennifer, the pastor of Sunnydale Church, with Dave and Betsy, a couple from the church, arrives at the training seminar on youth ministry with several questions. Youth ministry has not been healthy in their congregation for many years. The congregation remembers a time, however, when youth were everywhere in the church, attracted by a very active youth group. But lately at Sunnydale the youth group, when it meets, has only a few youth in attendance. Jennifer, Betsy, and Dave are hoping to get something going in youth ministry at their church. But they don't know where to start or how to get things going.

This book is an examination of youth ministry from a denominational and congregational perspective. I assume that the reader is interested in youth ministry within a congregational setting, although other organizations involved with youth—such as the Scouting movement, paradenominational groups, and nondenominational ministries (see chapter 8)—will be examined. I believe that youth ministry that operates from a congregational base is inherently different from youth ministry that operates outside the church. The core beliefs of a congregation, as well as denominational beliefs, will influence the development, leadership, program, and curriculum choices of the congregation's youth ministry. Thus I believe that one cannot overlook the history and structure of each congregation as it conceives and develops youth ministry to fit a particular understanding of ministry.

Most of the literature produced on youth ministry assumes a large, white, middle-class church structure and offers suggestions for developing an effective youth ministry within that privileged situation. This handbook is designed so that the steps outlined will work in urban churches or rural churches, small- or large-membership churches, and that each congregation will develop a youth ministry unique to its situation. I do not believe that there is a set formula for youth ministry that will "work" in every church setting. I do believe that by examining your church's unique ministry and by paying attention to the issues raised in this book, your church can develop an effective and *faithful* youth ministry.

Throughout the book, I have included some brief issues that Jennifer, Betsy, and Dave are struggling with. These questions are designed to help you think about the issues raised in this book and apply them to the youth ministry that engages your congregation. I hope to instill a spirit of continuous learning about youth ministry, because we are still discovering new ways to apply the gospel to the everyday lives of young people.

As you may be aware, youth ministry has been a key indicator of denominational decline (in both conservative and liberal groups) for more than twenty years. Many denominations have issued responses to the crisis. For example, The United Methodist Church has started a certification process in youth ministry, has revived national youth rallies, and has once again separated the youth curriculum department from the adult curriculum department. The Presbyterian Church (USA) has found monies for additional staffing at the national level. Seminaries have begun offering a variety of youth ministry courses, and several of the more conservative seminaries and colleges are offering degrees in youth work. While it is gratifying to see these new denominational developments, there is still much work to be done.

Part of the problem in denominational youth ministry today is a lack of clarity over what is meant by the term *youth*. We have been functioning with differing understandings of youth for more than two decades. So Dave, Betsy, and Jennifer might start by thinking about who they mean when they say they want to have a better youth ministry in their congregation. Who are the youth in youth ministry? Does "youth" mean a fifth grader, a drop-out from high school, a seventeen-year-old college student, or a juvenile delinquent who is incarcerated?

Age Categories

Most denominations typically define *youth* by age. Sometime in the early 1940s, most of the mainline Protestant denominations began to define youth as those people from age twelve to twenty-four. In time this definition was altered to include only young people from age twelve to eighteen. A new category called "young adults" was created for young people from eighteen to twenty-four years of age. Most of our denominational churches today define youth as those who are age twelve to eighteen.

This definition has some problems, however. When the age limits were set half a century ago, most young men and women did not reach puberty until after age twelve. This is no longer the case. While statistics vary, the average age for females to start their menstrual cycle is now below age twelve. Other hormonal changes normally associated with puberty for females take place well before menstruation and well before age twelve. It is not unusual, especially in large urban hospitals, to find girls under the age of twelve giving birth.[1]

Many of the groups doing research on the adolescent population (such as the Center for Early Adolescent Development and the Search Institute) are beginning to use age ten as the framework for a working definition of youth. This may be helpful, if we want to stay with age as the primary way we define youth.

I am not suggesting that we simply add all ten- and eleven-year-olds to the church's youth group. However, a specific ministry designed for this age group ought to be considered a part of the youth ministry. If we were to move in this direction, the youth ministry for those between the ages of ten and fourteen might be considerably different from the youth ministry for those over the age of sixteen.

There are also problems with the older end of the age definition. David Elkind has pointed out in his book *All Grown Up and No Place to Go* that American teenagers are maturing at an earlier and earlier age, only to find a society that wants them to wait longer and longer to assume full adult responsibilities, such as full-time, meaningful employment.[2] Indeed, some states discourage older teens (sixteen to eighteen) who want to drop out of school to get married and begin full-time employment by revoking their driver's licenses. The tremendous growth in both the numbers and the percentage of the adolescent population attending colleges and universities also attests to the issue that Elkind raises. A cynic might view college as a place where youth are told to wait another four years (perhaps five or six, depending on how quickly they do their college course work) before becoming adults and entering the work force full time.

While considering a working definition of youth, we need to remember that in many developing countries the term *youth* is used to describe anyone up to age thirty-five. At some international gatherings of youth, the delegates from these developing countries are older than the chaperons of delegates from the United States.

Some teens graduate from high school before they turn eighteen. Into what category of ministry does a seventeen-year-old college freshman fit? Should she or he be a part of the youth group or the adult program? Perhaps it is time to alter our perception of youth. The Carnegie Foundation prefers to label youth as persons from age ten to twenty, thus reflecting the cultural and biological changes young people experience today.[3]

Grade-Level Categories

Another way to categorize youth is by their grade level in school. Indeed, some programs are designed for "high-school ministry" or "junior-high ministry." Many churches use this criterion for youth ministry by focusing on grade-level groupings both in Sunday school and in youth fellowship groups. Parachurch groups, such as Young Life, and other organizations limit their ministry to youth from a particular high school.

This use of school as a determining criterion for grouping may extend to other parts of the church community as well. For example, when does a youth become eligible for the "adult" choir? When does a youth receive separate stewardship mailings and visitations? Many times, the answer is only after graduation from high school or college.

The problem with using school or the education model as a way to define youth is not in whom the definition includes (those in school) but in whom this definition excludes (those not in school). Educational revisionists suggest that over one million teens in this country are not in school. Newspapers lament the high and many-times increasing drop-out rate, especially in urban areas. Many teens are seeking some alternative to the traditional schooling pattern, which is prevalent in middle-class neighborhoods. The incarceration rate of teens in either jails or hospital rehabilitation programs continues to grow. This means that an increasing number of teens are not in what one would normally think of as school; however, churches still should minister to/with/by them.

A more practical problem is presented by the graded school definition of youth. How are we to organize our youth fellowship groups when each community seems to organize its schools differently? When the junior-high concept was started in the early part of this century, it was conceived for educational reasons. Today school groupings are made less often for educational reasons and more often for reasons involving space and size. Based on available space and size of particular grades, each school system makes a determination about how to group students in specific buildings. Thus middle school (not junior high anymore) may include grades five, six, seven, eight, or nine in a variety of configurations. We can no longer assume, if we ever could, that the same understanding of graded education persists in middle schools across North America. Those patterns that do emerge in each community may be changed from year to year, depending on the numbers of students in a particular class. This has often created awkward or unnatural groupings for the programmatic aspects of youth ministry.

Additionally, organizing youth ministry by grade level has left our traditionally "college aged" young people out of the picture. While some churches have developed a specialized ministry to those young people who have just graduated from high school, the majority have not. One must assume benevolently that church leaders believe that their ministry to adults will minister to and with these persons. Many of us know that this has not happened.

Despite these problems, the graded school understanding of youth ministry is beneficial for some congregations. For many youth, especially those from traditional middle-income or rural backgrounds, school and family are the dominant parts of their lives. The school can control from one third to one half of each teen's waking moments. Additionally, we as a society apparently think that all teens ought to be in high school. Thus the school can be a tremendous influence in the lives of teens and a very important part of youth ministry.

Most adult workers involved in youth ministry simply assume that school is a part of the life of youth. Thus books, programs, and conferences focus on high-school ministry or junior-high ministry. This pattern of youth ministry seems to "work" where the schooling patterns "work" in the American society. Where the schooling patterns are not working as well—namely, urban areas—in extreme rural areas and among minority groups, youth ministry that assumes school categories is not surprisingly performing poorly. The very way we understand and think about youth ministry in those areas is partly to blame for this "failure."

Church-Defined Categories

While school and age are the main categories used to define youth in our churches today, they are not the only factors. Unfortunately, some churches still consider youth only in terms of those on the rolls of the church or who happen to walk through the doors of the church. When these churches think about youth ministry, they do so only in terms of those whom the church family considers "theirs." These churches seem to have forgotten the universal aspect of ministry and God's saving grace.[4] Churches are called to be involved in the world, to minister to the community that surrounds them, not only to those youth who walk through their church doors or who are born to someone who is a member and gives money to the church structure.

Developmental Categories

Barbara Fuhrmann in *Adolescence, Adolescents* suggests a working definition of *adolescence:*

> the onset of puberty (at about 10 or 11 in girls, 12 or 13 in boys) to the assumption of full adult responsibilities: physical, social, legal and economic (usually about 21, but as early

19

as eighteen and as late as the mid-twenties or even thirties).
. . . Adolescence is "an open-ended period in which individuals character development defines the nature of the period" (Offer, 75, p. 180), with social, cultural, and historical factors exerting significant influence over the nature of that development.[5]

This definition makes sense from an academic standpoint, although it has many practical problems for the youth worker. Can we, for example, actually form a youth fellowship in terms of whether one has entered puberty? At this vulnerable age, too much stigma would result. However, as you examine your youth ministry you must begin struggling with the idea of who you are including or excluding in your program. We cannot expect our ministry to be effective or successful if we don't have an idea about the population to whom we want to minister.

The traditional age grouping of twelve to eighteen, which most church structures use, is not helpful, nor is the common definition of those in certain grade levels of school. Thus Betsy, Dave, and Jennifer should prefer to think of youth as beginning sometime around ten years old and ending when the youth are ready to accept full adult responsibilities, which may occur any time from about age sixteen to those leaving graduate schools in their mid or late twenties.

The next step is to focus on those youth they want to target in the ministry of their congregation. As the church— or as Jennifer, Dave, and Betsy—talks about those youth, a working definition of youth will become apparent.

Ministry to/with/by Youth

Now that we have examined the defining characteristics of youth, we should ponder the kind of ministry that is appropriate to your congregation.

Youth ministry is, of course, in part ministry to youth. All ministry is, at times, ministry to people and communities who are in some sort of distress and need. Youth ministry is particularly designed for this purpose.

Effective youth ministry has usually meant that adults are "doing" the ministry to youth. However, youth ministry is much more than doing something to youth. It is also ministry with youth. It is God's people, in community, nurturing and helping each other and others.

Effective youth ministry includes helping, nurturing, and working with individuals and the youth community as they grow and mature in their faith. Ministry with youth suggests that they are involved in the process of ministry, including decision-making processes, leadership tasks, and other responsibilities.

Further, youth ministry is accomplished by youth. God's people, including youth, are involved with ministry in God's creation. Youth are no exception to this. They can minister to the church community, to the wider community, to the adults working with the youth ministry, and to youth themselves. Often, adults working with youth need to get out of the way and let them use the gifts God has given them. Youth, no less than adults, can be ministers in the New Testament sense of the word.

At various times, the youth ministry of any congregation will have ministries to, with, and by youth. An effective and faithful youth ministry will include all three approaches to ministry.[6]

For our friends Dave, Betsy, and Jennifer, the idea of young people being in partnership with them in ministry is both exciting and terrifying. They are excited as they think about the possibilities of having the young people themselves help develop and carry out program and be involved in the ministry of the congregation. But it is terrifying to allow youth the opportunity to make decisions that may cause conflict or disagreement. It is threatening to think that they as adults are called to listen, really listen, to what teenagers may be saying about ministry. Further, if the members of the congregation's youth ministry have never been involved in a concept of ministry that includes them, they may rebel. It may be easier for the teenagers to allow adults to do all the work, all the planning, all the ministry than to get involved and help develop a ministry with and by youth.

Is youth ministry adult directed in your congregation? Or do young people and adults work side by side (ministry with youth)? Are there opportunities in your congregation's youth ministry for young people to be in ministry with the gifts that God has graced them with (ministry by youth)?

The Umbrella Concept

Youth ministry is not merely starting a youth fellowship or youth groups. Indeed, youth fellowships or youth groups are a particular form of youth ministry. Historically, fellowship groups started around the 1880s in the United States and have continued in some form into the present.[7] Many components might be involved in a youth ministry, including Sunday school classes, youth fellowship groups, choirs, athletic teams, Bible studies, and worship. Similarly, a church may have a very effective youth ministry and not have a particular part of youth ministry that another congregation has, such as a youth fellowship group. This book will discuss youth fellowship groups in some detail later, but will not be limited to an understanding of youth ministry as youth group. The image of an umbrella might be helpful.

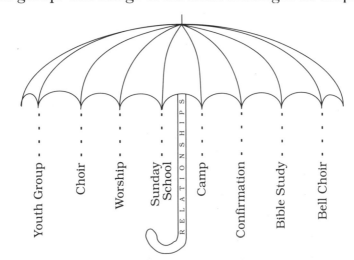

Youth Group · Choir · Worship · Sunday School · RELATIONSHIPS · Camp · Confirmation · Bible Study · Bell Choir

As the drawing suggests, relationships help to hold the differing programs together in any congregation's youth ministry.[8]

The umbrella concept is an exciting idea for Dave, Betsy, and Jennifer. They have always thought that ministering to/with/by youth means having a youth fellowship group. Now they can see how Sunday school classes, confirmation, choir, and worship may all be considered youth ministry. Further, they understand that a youth group is just one part of the congregation's youth ministry. They will look at their congregation in a new light.

YOUTH MINISTRY AUDIT

____ Youth fellowship groups (how many?)
____ Youth Sunday school classes (how many?)
____ Confirmation class
____ Choir
____ Youth-led worship
____ Bell choir
____ Athletic teams
____ Bible study
____ Summer camps
____ High adventure camps
____ Spiritual retreats
____ Scout troop
____ Support groups
____ Tutorial opportunities
____ Groups organized around talent or interest such
      as Book Club, Film Club
____ Youth newsletter
____ Youth musical

In what ways is your congregation already engaged in youth ministry? Take a moment to check the functions of youth ministry in your congregation.

Think About It Again

Jennifer, Betsy, and Dave now have some new ways of thinking about youth ministry as they head home from their first training session on youth ministry.

1. Who are the youth to be included in the youth ministry?
2. What are the differing ways of conceiving ministry to, with, and by youth?
3. How does their congregation's youth ministry already include these aspects of ministry, and how might they add new components to the congregation's youth ministry?
4. How does the umbrella concept help them to visualize all the differing aspects of youth ministry?

I hope that you are relieved to read that having great youth ministry does not necessarily mean that you have a great youth group. But do not give up hope that a great youth group can be an integral part of your youth ministry.

CHAPTER 2

Images for
Youth Ministry

Society is awash in images created in part by the print media, the film industry, and television. "The images cramming the consciousness of most today tend to be pre-set, borrowed images used in non-imaginative, literal ways to name and interpret life."[1] As I talk with congregations about youth ministry, I find that many people appear to have trouble imaging a youth ministry that they haven't participated in. While we live in a culture full of images, sometimes we have trouble creating them ourselves.[2] Here I will offer several images that I hope will be helpful as we examine youth ministry.

The images are not full-blown models. Hopefully, however, the images will begin to paint a picture that you will complete; perhaps suggesting a reality different from the one you understand or have participated in. The images that I am about to sketch are just that—sketches. They may ring true with your understanding of ministry to, with, and by adolescents, or they may ring hollow. One of the images might be the lens through which you see youth ministry, or it might be a lens you reject for theological or theoretical reasons. Please understand that I am not suggesting one unique image, but several—seven to be exact—because I believe that there is no single image for youth ministry, just as I believe that there is not a single model for effective, faithful youth ministry. I invite you to think of an image or two of your own that might help your congregation envision new ways of doing youth ministry.

The "Bill Cosby" Image

I call this the "Bill Cosby" image because Cosby had one of the top-rated television shows and because he is very good at what he does: entertain people. Using humor and real life, he often makes a valuable point. But if he doesn't, it really doesn't matter because we have been entertained. Students of mine have referred to this concept as babysitting image. It is not very popular with them, because these students believe that in it they are expected to merely babysit the youth, or entertain the kiddies. They think of a person, usually male, who has an ability to entertain with a guitar (some have called this "have guitar will travel"[3]) or with jokes or with words or with videos or with anything that holds the attention of the youth. One goal of this kind of ministry is to keep youth from being *bored*—that horrible possibility when one deals with adolescents. Of course, if the youth are not bored, they will continue to come to church, or at least to youth group. If one is a good enough entertainer, the youth ministry flourishes. And if one is a tremendous Christian entertainer, then Christian values, lifestyle, witness, and so on get infused within the entertainer's message.

The growing passivity of our culture is related to television, and perhaps an image from television can work for our youth ministry. However, those who believe that discipleship is an activity we engage in and not one in which we passively sit back to be entertained will find this image unhelpful and not what we believe youth ministry is about. But a church may try to be a Bill Cosby, hire a Bill Cosby stand-in, or want the youth leader to be Bill Cosby.

The "Merlin the Magician" Image

This is one of my favorite images, in part because Merlin the Magician was always my fairy-tale hero. The man would appear almost magically and mysteriously to solve the problems facing King Arthur and his kingdom. Then Merlin disappeared, only to be summoned again or to appear in another time of crisis. Some churches appear to expect Merlin to mysteriously arrive and solve or deal with their youth ministry problem. This image, too, gets a lot of negative publicity unless you are Merlin or your congregation has summoned Merlin. Part of this negative reaction is that when Merlin leaves, no one else in the congregation understands anything more about ministry or youth ministry than they did before. Enabling laity to do youth ministry or enabling youth to minister is not what this image is about. Typically the Merlin person has a tremendous charismatic gift of helping groups, such as youth groups, come alive and become excited about ministry and life.

I have some sympathy for this image because in reflecting on my own ministry, I see that I have been like Merlin. Arriving at a congregation at the wave of a denominational leader's wand or simply because I live near a particular church while I teach at a seminary, I begin a ministry with adolescents. A few years or even months later, I am whisked away, leaving a flourishing youth ministry that may not survive without me.[4] That church may not be ready to assume the youth ministry that was being done in "their" name.

Some of you may see these two images, the "Bill Cosby" entertainer and the Merlin the Magician, as closely related. You are right; they are. Yet, there are some differences. Entertainers do what they do best—entertain. Magicians do what they do best—"magically" solve an immediate problem. I believe these two images are what many churches are looking for in youth ministry. Unfortunately, this under-standing of ministry is extremely limited.

The "Anne Sullivan" Image

As you may know, as a child Helen Keller was struck by a disease that left her blind, deaf, and unable to speak. In the spring of 1887, Anne Mansfield Sullivan was employed by Helen's family to try to teach her. For several months Anne worked with Helen, trying to enable her to spell rudimentary words by making finger signs on Helen's palm. Then a breakthrough came in the life of Helen Keller, the "aha!" experience, the "teachable moment," or if your theology prefers, the movement of the Holy Spirit. Helen Keller described the experience years later in her autobiography:

> We—Helen and Anne—walked down the path to the well-house, attracted by the fragrance of the honey suckle with which it was covered. Someone was drawing water and my teacher placed my hand under the spout. As the cool stream gushed over one hand, she spelled into the other the word water, first slowly and then rapidly. I stood still, my whole attention fixed upon the motions of her fingers. Suddenly I felt a misty consciousness as of something forgotten—a thrill of returning thought; and somehow the mystery of language was revealed to me. I knew then that w-a-t-e-r meant that wonderful cool something that was flowing over my hand. That living word awakened my soul, gave it light, hope, joy, set it free! There were barriers still, it is true, but barriers that could in time be swept away. I left the well-house eager to learn. Everything had a name, and each name gave birth to a new thought. As we returned to the house every object which I touched seemed to quiver with life. . . . It would have been difficult to find a happier child than I was as I lay in my crib at the close of that eventful day and lived over the joys it had brought me, and for the first time I longed for a new day to come.[5]

It is important to see the extent to which Annc Sullivan's presence made possible Helen Keller's discovery. Anne Sullivan did not cause the learning to occur, but her presence with Helen throughout all the tedious weeks of dealing with simple signs established a possibility that otherwise would have been missing. She was with Helen as an image of what could be hoped for. She had no presumptions about her ability to teach Helen Keller, but she knew what conditions might be created in which this learning might take place. She maintained the continuity of Helen's instruction, and she was ready to interact with her when the teachable moment occurred. Furthermore, she understood that this particular breakthrough was only a starting point. But she realized clearly that it was from this point that Helen Keller's education could truly begin.[6]

Is this a helpful image for youth ministry? We, in the church, are establishing a possibility with our youth, building a relationship with them, so that when the Holy Spirit moves within them or when the "aha!" experience happens, we are present and ready to seize the opportunity, realizing that this is just the start of the faith pilgrimage. Can we be to youth what Anne Sullivan was to Helen Keller, an image of what can be hoped for?

For many years these three images alone were my idea of youth ministry, with the latter being the one I held the most hope for in terms of youth ministry. Recently, however, I have begun to find four other images useful.

The Storm Home Image

"Minnesota blizzards, Garrison Keillor recalls from his youth, often attacked without notice, stranding farm kids in town where they attended high school. Knowing this danger, school officials would assign each pupil a 'storm home.' "[7] A kind, caring, and loving family would volunteer to take in students until the roads were cleared enough for them to go home.

Can this be a useful image for youth ministry in a local congregational setting? Is the church a place where a safe haven, a storm home if you will, ought to be provided for teens, a refuge from the "storms" of their adolescent years?

The church's youth ministry may need to provide a home for youth safe from the ravages of a drug culture or gang wars that may be occurring in the neighborhoods in which they live. Or the church may need to be a place for youth caught between two cultures, the world of their immigrant parents and their new home of America. The church may need to be a place where second-generation Americans can come and relax, being themselves without fear of rejection or tension with either of the two cultures they live in daily. Additionally, the church's youth ministry may be helpful to those adolescents who find their family home a place of abuse. The church's ministry with youth may need to be composed of warm, kind, caring, and loving adults who incarnate God's love in a family or community atmosphere.

Recently I ran into a former student of mine on the streets of Chicago. She is serving a church in inner-city Detroit. Her question to me was why hadn't the seminary prepared her to deal with how to keep guns and drugs out of church, how to deal with the gang whose "turf" was across the street from her church, or her fifth grader who is a local drug supplier. Would a "storm home" youth ministry be an appropriate image for her church's youth ministry?

"Julie, the White-Water Rafting Guide" Image

Julie is a white-water rafting guide whom we got to know over the past several summers as we rafted with her down rivers in North Carolina. Her task was to gently guide us down a stretch of river that she had navigated before. Each day the river was different, and each group that went with her had its own personality and problems. No two trips were ever the same for her. She thought of herself as feeling her way down the river with the other people in her raft. She envisioned herself as an enabler and empowerer of the people in the raft—so that before the trip was over, the people in the raft were in control of the trip. Although at times she would strongly suggest to us a particular way of navigating, she never demanded that we had to do things her way. Rather, her attitude was "Here is the river of life; let us journey down the river together, as partners, each of whom brings special and unique gifts to the journey and to our raft."

Is this a helpful image of youth ministry leaders, as guides, rafting down the river of life with all its rapids and calm eddies with youth? If this image is our guide, we do not tell youth where to go; rather, we go with them, making mistakes with them and showing them parts of the river they may never see for themselves. We try to keep the journey relatively safe, but we know that being on the river means that some safety is sacrificed. We know that letting youth make decisions means some safety is sacrificed, but we also know that is the way youth can learn and be empowered for life.

The Worship Image

Don Webb is the retired President of Centenary College in Shreveport, Louisiana. He was my pastor during part of my adolescent years and was one of the people who opened up for me the whole world of worship. He helped to make worship come alive, to have meaning, to become a central part of my life. Worship as an image for youth ministry is a brief sketch I would like us to entertain.

In some churches, one of which William Myers identifies in his recent book, *Black and White Styles of Youth Ministry*,[8] worship is the central part of their experience together. From worship flows the entire life of the congregation. In this church, the entire youth ministry, as well as all other ministries, flows from the liturgical experience of Sunday morning. Worship is alive, a pulsating experience that youth not only participate in but also help to lead with regularity. The reason I sketch this image in the terms of an example is that we have yet to see it work for any length of time in white, middle-class, mainline churches. Worship for youth in many churches is a deadening and life-sapping experience that holds no meaning or relevance for youth and the world in which they live. However, William Myers has proved to me the possibilities of this image, and so I lift it up with some hope that perhaps you can use it in your congregation's youth ministry.[9] Don Webb succeeded in making worship the central part of my life as an adolescent.

The Artist Image

Michael Warren describes the artist image this way:

> The question I love to ask teachers is: Tell me about the special talents of the young people you meet. One can answer that question only by pointing to particular persons. One has to name individuals and then explain how one has been paying attention to their strengths rather than to their weaknesses. This amounts to a connoisseurship of the human, an aesthetic sensitivity to human beauty and possibility. For any of us to do this, we must have the eye of an artist, which is the eye of a lover. . . . Sometimes I think that every young person is a virtuoso-in-secret and that my role is to discover the virtuosity.[10]

Can we as a church, as adults in the church, be artists, seeing in each youth the special gifts and talents and graces that they have been blessed with by God?[11] This image empowers youth for ministry. It is able to bring careful consideration of the gifts that God has given to people for youth ministry. This image may call us to take vocation seriously once again in youth ministry, helping youth to discover and build a vocation around their gifts and talents and not around wealth, prestige, power, or some other cultural understanding of success.

I have offered seven images for youth ministry, two of which may tell us what things are like (Bill Cosby and Merlin the Magician), and five that may call us to what youth ministry could be like (Anne Sullivan, Julie the white-water guide, the artist, worship, and the storm home images). I know that I have not exhausted the images. For example, Jeff Johnson has sketched an image of youth ministry as evangelization, "of inviting persons into deeper relationships with us, with themselves, with their God,"[12] and, I might add with God's creation. Perhaps you have other images that are helpful for you in your unique situation. I have sketched these images, not to fully explain them or for you to understand them as models of youth ministry. Rather, I want to lift up some images of what might be possible for your congregation in its ministry with, to, and by adolescents.

For Jennifer, Betsy, and Dave, whom we met in chapter 1, these images were helpful as they began to think about youth ministry at Sunnydale Church. Jennifer commented that she often thought of herself as the ringmaster of a seven-ring circus. Betsy agreed that the hectic pace of congregational life often made her feel that way, too. They also thought that some of the people who helped to govern the church didn't have any vision of what youth ministry could be at Sunnydale. They began to think about what image or combination of images fit best with what they wanted to happen at Sunnydale in youth ministry. What images resonated with you? Why? Does one of the images describe things at your church better than the other images? Are there other images that you want to use to describe or suggest youth ministry in your church? What is the most helpful image for you as you think about youth ministry?

CHAPTER 3

Key Ingredients
for Effective and Faithful
Youth Ministry

Jennifer, Dave, and Betsy were anticipating the second session of their youth ministry training session, as the speaker had promised to address the "secret" of congregational youth ministry. They really wanted to know what made for successful youth ministry in other churches around the country.

There can be little doubt that "effective youth ministry" is a major concern of both pastors and laypersons.[1] While what constitutes effective youth ministry can be debated endlessly, four key ingredients constitute "effective" and "faithful" youth ministry from a congregational perspective.

Intentional Ministry

Congregations ought to have intentions, definite plans, purposes, goals, and objectives toward which energy and resources can be mobilized. Ministry must be, at times, a reaction, such as reacting to a death or to a crisis. But ministry should also be thoughtful planning and attention to what God and the church are called to be and to do. Congregational youth ministry is responding to God's call in the individual and collective lives of the congregation.

Intentional youth ministry develops a clearly understood purpose with goals and objectives. While most major denominations have formulated some sort of purpose statement for "their" youth ministry, each congregation needs to struggle with its own specific intentions for its youth ministry to be effective and faithful.

Dean Hoge and some of his colleagues did a survey of youth ministers and parents of teenagers, representing six denominations, identifying their intended goals for youth ministry. The survey called for educators and parents from various different denominations to rank the sixty given items in order of preference for the intentions of youth ministry. The results point to several issues that are crucial in determining a congregation's intentions for youth ministry.

Of the sixty items, the number-one priority for youth ministry over the entire survey was that youth should have "a healthy self-concept about their value and worthiness as a person." While this was the overall highest priority, when the survey was examined denominationally, two denominations did not agree with this assessment. For the Southern Baptist and Church of God educators and parents, having "a personal relationship with Jesus Christ" was the number-one priority for youth ministry.[2]

There are two important points to be made about Dean Hoge's survey. The first is not which priority is the best, but that different people, congregations, and denominations can and do view the intentions of youth ministry differently. Indeed, they ought to be viewed differently. Thus a key question that must be answered by each congregation is this: What are your congregation's intentions in youth ministry? Do you intend

- to have youth set an example of Christian behavior?
- for youth to have a faith life that holds meaning in the everyday world?

- for youth to develop a personal relationship with Jesus or the triune God?
- for youth to have a healthy self-concept?
- to help "youth to grow spiritually"?[3]
- to have youth attend worship or youth group?

All of these goals may be considered faithful intentions of youth ministry, but each person, congregation, and denomination will give priority to these goals in a different order or manner.

Congregational youth ministry may be able to sustain several intentions at once, but sooner or later priority attention must be given to just a few. Once a congregation has decided which direction to take in youth ministry, a comprehensive vision of youth ministry and how it can be accomplished can be carried out.

Think back on chapter 2 and the different images of youth ministry presented there. Each image has a predominant intention for youth ministry. Most of us respond to one image more than to another precisely because our intentions, our understanding of the goals of youth ministry, differ.

Further, each individual local church is different from the composite of its denominational tendencies. So you may or may not agree with the results of Hoge's survey. The point is not which intention is "more appropriate" or better than the other. Rather, we must realize that various different intentions are legitimately a part of youth ministry. Your church and you must begin to have some intentions for youth ministry to be truly effective.

The second important learning from the survey is that educators (youth ministers) and parents can have vastly different intentions for youth ministry. For example, one of the highest priorities of youth ministry for parents across denominational lines was that youth should cooperate with parents, school, and church authorities. However, the educators never viewed this as one of their top priorities for youth ministry. Thus parents and youth ministers may have vastly different ideas about what youth ministry should be about. And remember that parents and educators represent just two parts of local congregational life. Other members of the congregation may have still different ideas about what is important in youth ministry.

Differences within the congregation around the intentions or ideas for youth ministry need to be acknowledged and discussed so that compromises and a cohesive vision can be articulated and then implemented.

I can still remember a conversation I had with several concerned parents who felt that my job as youth minister was to provide fun activities for their youth to attend under the auspices of the church. However, with the support of the youth council, I had initiated a spiritual growth segment into this church's youth ministry. The parents wanted only fun and games, but the youth wanted something more substantial.

Here is another example of what we have been discussing. A national gathering of youth from a mainline denomination takes place each summer on the beach. The expressed purpose of this gathering is to lead youth to a relationship with Jesus Christ—a worthy goal. The group's own research suggests that over 95 percent of the youth attending already profess to have, before they come to the event, a personal and meaningful relationship with Jesus Christ. And many of the youth who attend this event continue to return, even after they are out of the "youth" category. The national gathering could be more effective and faithful, I believe, if it helped the youth grow in their relationship with Jesus Christ. This is a different intention and would be approached differently than trying to bring youth to a relationship with Jesus Christ.

Another example: Leaders in a large church in the South, with over 2,000 members, could not understand why only sixteen or so youth were involved in the Sunday school and fellowship parts of their youth ministry. It became obvious in our discussions together that the adult workers with youth in the church were nearly equally divided on what their intentions should be in youth ministry. Half believed that a personal relationship with Jesus Christ was the purpose of youth ministry, and half wanted to help the youth develop positive images of themselves. Now both intentions are excellent, but these adult workers with youth were at odds with each other over these intentions. Both intentions could probably be accomplished at this church, but not until the problem was recognized, negotiated, and dealt with in a positive spirit of working together.

Final Word on Intentions

I am convinced that four types of people need to be involved in the formulating of the purposes, goals, and objectives of youth ministry. These are the leaders of the congregation (or the "power" people in a congregation if they are not the elected leaders); the parents of the youth who are or could be involved; the youth themselves; and the adult workers with youth, those whom the church hopes to take the leadership in accomplishing its intentions. It is only as this mix of people in the local setting sit down and carefully think through what they wish youth ministry to be about that youth ministry can be tailored for each particular setting. Further, it is as each local church gathers people together to discuss their intentions in youth ministry that the church, its leaders, and its youth leaders can become committed and can commit the resources of the congregation to youth ministry.

As a purpose statement, with refined goals and objectives, is created by people in local settings, other issues will surface, such as allocation of resources, including finances, leadership, and space; planning; theological assumptions; and biblical understandings. As people in the local setting struggle with these issues, make conscious decisions about

SOME POSSIBLE GOALS FOR YOUTH MINISTRY

1. Youth will have a healthy self-concept about their value and worthiness as a person.
2. Youth will set an example of Christian behavior.
3. Youth will grow in their faith.
4. Youth will have a personal relationship with Jesus Christ.
5. Youth will attend worship.
6. Youth will provide church leadership.
7. The church will provide youth a safe haven from the outside world.
8. Youth will explore life vocations from the aspect of God's calling in their lives.
9. Youth will identify themselves as Christians and act accordingly.
10. Youth will explore how to build Christian community by participating in one.
11. Youth and the church will begin to create a better world with God's help.
12. Youth will begin an active prayer life.
13. Youth will have experienced the gift of tongues.
14. Youth will have knowledge of the Christian tradition.
15. Youth will have knowledge of world religions.
16. Ten adults in the congregation will know each youth by name.
17. *
18.
19.
20.

* What other goals would you add? How would you prioritize this list?

them, and attempt to carry them out that youth ministry will become truly intentional in character and form.

This means that the youth ministry at First Church may be quite similar or very different from youth ministry in an urban parish or a rural setting or even in the church across the street. This means that some youth ministries that "work" or are "successful" in one place may not work in another, as the intentions of each congregation may be different. Certain congregations are going to have specific intentions that are not appropriate for all congregations.

For example, many Korean-American congregations will need to deal with the issue of parental authority in a vastly different way from other congregations because of the nature of the family structure in Korea and in North America. Black congregations may want to specifically focus on black males and issues of identity that are not appropriate for white congregations. Rural congregations may have a vastly different agenda from that of growing suburban congregations.

Relational Ministry

Youth ministry, understood as relationship—a bond that exists between the leader and the youth—is not new. However, in many cases the idea of relational ministry is under stood strictly in terms of the relationship between the adult workers with youth and the youth themselves.

The concept of youth ministry as being limited to the relationship between the adult worker with youth and the youth themselves *can be* destructive. Some charismatic adult workers with youth use relational ministry to create a group that focuses on adult leadership. The ministry points to the adult workers themselves and not beyond them to the church and to the Triune God. When this happens, the youth ministry is in trouble.

Similarly, some adult workers with youth or youth themselves discover that a quick way to build a sense of purpose and cohesiveness is to unite against a common enemy. The "common enemy" that unites the group can be either the church or parents. Occasionally the scenario is played out where other youth, the society in which the youth live, or the senior pastor—and in some cases, even the youth worker—become the enemy.

I maintain that youth ministry, as all other ministries, is inherently relational, people incarnating the love of God. It is God's people reaching out to God's creation, just as God reaches out to God's creation. Adult workers with youth need to develop positive adult friendships with youth. Chapter 4 includes a discussion on how to develop strong, healthy relationships between adult workers with youth and the youth involved in that ministry.

The idea of relational ministry in youth ministry includes at least three main relationships besides the relationship of the adult workers with youth. They are (1) the relationship between God and youth; (2) the relationship between youth and the "created order"; and (3) the relationship between youth and God's gift, the church.

The Relationship Between Youth and God

Youth ministry is, in a very real sense, concerned with the relationship between the young person and God, understood in God's triune fullness. The adolescent years are a perfect time, developmentally, to examine the issue of God's coming to human beings as one fully human and yet fully divine, Jesus the Christ. Some have, rightly so, pushed the concept of Jesus as a friend to youth. However, we can become too Christ-centered in our ministry. By this I mean that Christ becomes God, and we, in effect, end up worshiping Christ—making Jesus into an idol—and not God in God's fullness, whom we of the Christian faith have affirmed as the Triune God.

While recognizing that no adult can be fully responsible for the relationship that does or does not exist between youth and God, youth ministry needs to be involved in helping young people create, explore, examine, and strengthen their relationship with God. Youth ministry needs to be involved with challenging youth in their faith and assisting them to mature in their relationship with God.

The Relationship Between Youth and the Created Order

Youth ministry is concerned with the relationship between youth and God's creation. The term "created order" refers to all of God's creation. Thus the relationships between youth and their family—parents, siblings, extended family—and other youth are all included in this category. And relational ministry goes beyond youth and their families to youth and God's creation. The world includes other people as well as the earth itself. Obviously this is a very comprehensive arena.

Many writers and thinkers have helped us to understand the young person's quest for identity. Youth are involved in some way in that process all of their teen years. Relational youth ministry ought to be involved in working with youth and their image of themselves, helping them to understand the image of God, in which they are created. Thus relational youth ministry helps youth to relate to God, to the church, to God's creation—both human and nonhuman—and to themselves.

Youth, no less than anyone else in society, are in relationships with God's creation. How they respond and act toward that creation is a large part of what being part of God's community is all about. It is essential that youth ministry be involved with helping youth deal with God's creation, both human and otherwise, in a faithful manner.

The Relationship Between Youth and God's Gift, the Church

Those of us who come at youth ministry from a congregational or church base need to remember the church.

Youth are called to be in relationship with God, but they are also called to be in relationship with a body of disciples, a body of believers. The church was and is God's gift to us as Christians.

In many circles a debate rages over whether the church is necessary. Sometimes the debate centers around whether the church is necessary for salvation. Some people proclaim, "I'm a good Christian, even though I don't participate in or belong to a church."

One of the misunderstandings we have in North American Christianity is the idea that while the church is a good idea, we really don't need it. Individualism runs rampant in our culture. Any understanding of tradition or scripture suggests that the church is very necessary for Christians. While it may not be a condition for salvation, youth need to be connected with a body of believers—a church—who can help nurture them, assist them, and challenge them to help others in the community of believers in a similar manner.

Programmatic Ministry

Youth ministry needs to have content in addition to relationships and intentionality. Michael Warren, a well-known Roman Catholic educator, has called relational ministry the "contact" part of youth ministry and the programmatic area the "content" part of youth ministry.[4] Both areas are important. Program is a part of youth ministry, but not all of youth ministry. A well-conceived programmatic ministry can, in conjunction with a ministry of intentionality and relationships, attract and involve youth in sizable numbers and in Christian growth.

Program is never "the answer." Those who opt for this view often end up writing books of "canned" programs or training youth "professionals" to insert a new program without an understanding of the local setting or any of the other factors that need to be taken into account for a program to be "effective." I want to spend some time discussing how to build a strong programmatic component of youth ministry, but I will save that discussion for the next chapter.

During a break in their session, our friends Betsy, Dave, and Jennifer began to think about the difference between a programmatic and a relational understanding of youth ministry. They asked these questions of themselves and their church's youth ministry: Has our youth ministry been focused strictly on program to the exclusion of relationships? Has our youth ministry been focused strictly on relationships without any meaningful program or content?

Faithfulness, or Gospel, Ministry

Youth ministry ought to be "faithful." Youth ministry from a congregational perspective assumes a Christian community and a Christian context. The very reason why we as a church, or as Christians, are about youth ministry is to be faithful. Unfortunately, the Christian community has been divided upon how an individual Christian is to be faithful in the world.

For example, look at the Christian response to abortion. While few Christian groups openly endorse abortion, the Christian church has been divided about how a Christian should respond to the issue of abortion. People on either side of the abortion debate have trouble understanding or even believing that those on the opposite side are really Christians. Despite the problems in knowing how to act in a faithful manner, we who are involved in youth ministry need to attempt to be faithful. While one cannot spell out all of what it means to be faithful, several issues appear to be extremely important in exploring what it means to be faithful in youth ministry.

Speak the Truth in Love (Ephesians 4:15a)

Frederick Buechner said it well when he wrote:

> Let the preacher tell the truth. The Gospel is bad news before it is good news. It is the news that man is a sinner. . . . That is a tragedy. But it is also the news that he is loved anyway, cherished, forgiven, bleeding to be sure, but also bled for. This is the comedy. . . . And just as in fairy tales extraordinary things happen. It is impossible for anybody to leave behind the darkness of the world he carries on his back like a snail, but for God all things are possible. That is the fairy tale. All together they are the truth. But to preach the Gospel is not just to tell the truth but to tell the truth in love, and to tell the truth in love means to tell it with concern not only for the truth that is being told but with concern for the people it is being told to.[5]

Youth ministry must tell the truth for it to be faithful. It must be centered in the Christian story and present that story in all of its ambiguities. The Christian story is both complex and simple. It is at the same time the story we know so well, and the story that has been forgotten.

Some youth ministries are very effective in presenting one part of the gospel. They specialize in evangelism or social action or nurture or discipleship. It is not that they don't present the gospel; rather, they present only a narrow part of the gospel. What is needed is for youth ministry to realistically and honestly present the whole gospel. Young people need to be called to make a commitment to Christ, to be challenged to do something about their faith, as well as to be nurtured in their faith.

Youth ministry must be biblically based and theologically centered. For far too long we have obscured the truth. The whole gospel needs to be proclaimed. The truth needs to be told.

The "Unthinkable" (Proclaiming Hope)

Beth A. Richardson expresses what many young people are struggling with. "The Unthinkable" is becoming a part of our consciousness: We could be destroyed in a nuclear holocaust.[6] The research done on early adolescence by the Search Institute bears out what Richardson expressed in her prose.[7] For some youth, there is no hope of a future that they will participate in and be a part of. Youth ministry must proclaim hope in the face of ultimate destruction, whether that destruction comes from lack of jobs, hunger, or a nuclear accident.

For some communities, such as portions of the community of black adolescent males, there is little to be hopeful about. The unemployment rate is unbelievably high, the crime rate is astronomical, and the hope for a better tomorrow is almost nonexistent. Into this reality, youth ministry must proclaim a hope that is real.

The Undoable

Grant Shockley, in the Miller-Fondren Lectures at Scarritt, suggested that the youth group is one of the most racially segregated parts of the church and of society.[8] Is this faithful? Is this the gospel?

For too long in youth ministry we have debated and perhaps even participated in activities designed to break down the barriers of prejudice and racial segregation. These attempts have done little, if anything, to break down the barriers of racial exclusion in our churches or our communities. We have not transformed the world but have been conformed by it. And even as I write this, I know of many youth ministries that think racism is not an issue that the church ought to be involved with, or that racism is not a problem in our culture.

The Unbelievable

Many Christians cannot understand that the United States is now a pluralistic society and that the United States shelters a multitude of religious beliefs and values. Yet youth ministry must engage young people in the task of living as Christians in a pluralistic society. It has to help young people understand the world community and the way they as Christians are called to relate to the world.

Basil Karp states that "several recent studies have shown that young Americans are woefully unprepared for the new global circumstances."[9] Those in leadership positions in youth ministry—both adults and youth—must become educated to the growing interdependency of the global society and the increasingly pluralistic society in which we all live. Youth ministry must participate in the shaping of a new way of life that acknowledges global interdependence and our pluralistic society.

Certainly there are other aspects to being a faithful Christian in today's world. Each denomination and each congregation has traditions about what issues and concerns are the most important. This is how each congregation lives out its commitment to God. I have mentioned just a few areas that I believe are important for a local congregation to be involved with if one is to remain faithful. The issue of sexuality, the call of discipleship, and developing Christian leaders are all arenas that we ought to take into account as we look at what it means to be faithful. Too often churches don't examine the whole gospel in their attempt to do youth ministry.

In workshops that I lead, in classes that I teach, and in discussions I find a consistent theme that can be called the search for the "secret" of congregational youth ministry. Everyone wants to find the elusive secret so that they can then do youth ministry effectively and quickly. John L. Parker, Jr., in a novel entitled *Once a Runner,* explores this theme from a different perspective:

Over the course of several years at Southeastern as his fame grew, many undergraduate runners sought him out as a training partner, thinking to pick up on the Secret. Expecting all manner of horrific exertion, they were generally stunned and giddy to find they could so easily make it through one of Denton's calendar days. Showing up the second morning they were of good cheer, perhaps trying to imagine how they would handle the pressure of fame. The second day also went well, but they would begin to notice something peculiar. There was no let up. . . . On the third day his outlook began to bleaken. For one thing, he was getting tired. Very tired. No particular day wore him out, but the accumulation of steady mileage began to take its toll. He never quite recovered fully between workouts and soon found himself walking around in a more or less constant state of fatigue—depression. . . . The new runner would find it more tedious than he could bear. The awful truth dawned: there was no Secret![10]

The secret of youth ministry, if it can be called that, is the constant, almost tedious, attention to the aspects of youth ministry that I have discussed. The persevering presence of the church as represented by its people, God's people, is the secret of youth ministry. I am convinced that through patient attention to the different aspects of youth ministry—intentional, relational, programmatic, and gospel—youth ministry will become truly effective in a local church setting.

The truth must be spoken. And it must be the whole truth. The truth must not be watered down or sugarcoated or obscured by our politics or theology. The truth must be spoken in love—love for the truth, for those for whom we speak, and for ourselves.

Jennifer, Betsy, and Dave felt overwhelmed by all the work they would need to do in their congregation as they left the second training session. They had come hoping for a quick, easy solution (the secret), and they left realizing all the weeks of work that lay ahead. But they also left with a sense of hope. They had a sense of direction. They were going to pull together a group at the church and focus on the intentions for youth ministry. At the same time, they realized that they needed to combine a programmatic and relational ministry.

Perhaps by now you can see more clearly how in different congregations youth ministry could be very different and yet still be effective. The way each congregation will respond to being faithful will be different. What each congregation decides as its intentions may be different, the content of the program may be different, and the nature of the relationships will be different. However, if each congregation focuses on its intentions, its relationships, its program, and its faithfulness, youth ministry will be effective and "successful."

CHAPTER 4

Building
Strong Relationships

Jennifer, Dave, and Betsy had been excited by the idea of including a relational ministry along with the programmatic ministry their congregation had already begun. But they were a little uncertain of how to get started, or what a relational ministry might look like.

The heart of youth ministry is relationships, just as the heart of the church is the relationships developed among its members and between each member and God. For too long, churches have forgotten or ignored the building of relationships between adult members and youth. While programs are important, a significant part of youth ministry is about relationships and building a relational ministry.

As I said in the previous chapter, there are many relationships in a relational ministry, but one of the key relationships is between the adults of the church and the youth of the church. Many adults are unclear as to how one develops relationships with youth. The easiest way to build rapport with a teen is the same way one develops any relationship—by spending time together, by sharing interests, and by having common concerns. As adults and youth spend time together, sharing mutual interests, talking with each other (which is not adults talking at youth), and taking each other seriously, relationships begin to develop. These relationships do take some time to develop, and it is only as the adults and teens have this time together that a relational ministry can succeed.

It is helpful to remember that the concept of time for a teenager is different from an adult's conception. While adults tend to see time in terms of years, teenagers tend to see time in terms of months or even weeks. Thus a two-year friendship between an adult and a teenager can seem to the teenager as a lifelong bond. This explains why some adults can develop deep friendships with teens in the space of several months. Unfortunately few churches have adults who will take the time and commit the energy to developing lasting friendships with teens.

In our culture most teens have very few, if any, adults who really know them. The continued urbanization and suburbanization of the country has established concentrated places where teens gather. Large consolidated high schools have also created the situation where teens spend most of their time with other teens. Contact with adults, especially with a broad age range of adults, has been minimized. Never before in our history have so many teens been concentrated in such a small space with so few adults to watch over them. This is one of the reasons why it is imperative for youth in today's society to have adult friends who know them. These adult friends can help teens in times of questioning, in times of trouble, and in times of joy.

In many places, including our church communities, there is a lack of adult role models. This problem is extremely significant in many of the ethnic communities in our country, especially the African-American community. The problem is intensified by the fact that in many churches the most active members are female.[1]

It is often difficult to find any adults who are willing to take the time and energy that is needed to invest in a congregation's youth ministry. Nevertheless the challenge of youth ministry is to recruit and educate adults who are willing to spend time and commit their energy to being with young people.

As you are developing congregational youth ministry, here are some hints for building relationships with young people.

Basic Data Gathering

One of the keys in building relationships is knowing something about these teens you are in relationship with. Gather information such as when the teen was born (a birthday card is nice to send); siblings; divorced parents and/or visitation issues; whether the teen works and, if so, where and when he or she works; other activities the teen participates in, such as band, athletics, drama club. Having the teen's current phone number and address is crucial. It always amazes me how much a simple birthday card or a note received at summer camp can mean to a teen. Whatever gifts and talents the teen has is another helpful piece of information to know, as you may be able to encourage the teen to use her or his gift or talent for God. For example, perhaps the youth can participate in worship. Can she read out loud well? Can he play a musical instrument? Will she pray before a large group? Does he have carpentry skills for a work camp? Are the teens interested in athletics but are not good enough to be on the high school team and would love to play on a church league team? Or are they into journalism and can help with the youth newsletter?

I usually keep this kind of information on an index card. I also keep track of it when I make a personal visit with the teen, so I can make sure all the teens are being called on. A sample of my index card appears on the next page.

Be Yourself

Most teens can tell whether you are putting on an act to get close to them or just pretending to be their friend. You

Name _____

Phone _____

Address _____

Age _____

Birthday _____

School Grade _____

Family Situation _____

Hobbies _____

Work _____

Address and Phone _____

Tidbits _____

Record of Contacts (on back) _____

must be yourself, which at times can be harder to do than we think, as many of us are not in tune with who we really are in the first place. You cannot relate to every teen. This is one of the reasons why it is important to have a variety of adults working with the congregation's youth ministry. To be overly simplistic, one doesn't want all "jocks or cheerleader types" working with the youth ministry but a variety of adults with a variety of interests. You can relate to those teens who have similar interests and perspectives to yours. A congregational youth ministry ought to have a variety of adults who are willing to enter into a relationship with teens. These adults, in part because of their variety of interests, will be able to find teens who are willing to spend time with them.

In those churches where only a few adults are involved in the youth ministry, it is imperative that those adults be open to a variety of young people. It may be even more important that these adults keep track of their contact with the teens, so that they can be sure all of the teens have been visited and that the adults know all of the teens in the ministry program.

I recommend that most congregational youth ministry programs assign different adults to each youth so that the adults can develop long-term and helpful personal relationships with the teens in the congregational youth ministry. Most adults will find some teens whom they enjoy being with or talking to. It is important as an adult worker with youth for you to be willing to listen, to be nonjudgmental, to have the time, to like being with them, and to be able to share a faith perspective. (See the next chapter, on adult leaders with youth).

Respect Confidentiality

The main barrier between adults and teens is often the issue of trust and confidentiality. Many times youth will share something with an adult to test whether the adult can be trusted with the information, whether the adult will tell the teen's parents or other symbol of authority. Too many times adult leaders with youth do not keep confidences. The only time information ought to be shared is when a life is in danger. If you get in a position where you feel you must share the information with somebody, you may want to seek permission of the youth before you act. This can help to maintain the teen's trust in you and deepen your relationship with the teen.

I'm not sure I can overemphasize this point. *Teens need to have adults they can trust.* They need adults with whom they can share their deepest feelings and concerns. In most cases, if the teens haven't shared this information with their parents, it is because the relationship the teens have with their parents is not very sound. Your sharing of what the teen has entrusted to you with their parents is not going to improve the communication and relationship the teen has with his or her parents. In many cases, it will only exacerbate the problem.

Key on Common Interests

Like most adult relationships, the relationship adults have with teens will focus on common interests. So what are the common interests you, as an adult, have with the teens you are establishing relationships with? (See topics at the end of the chapter for a way to get started in your conversations with teens.)

I love music and find that music is a way into the teen's world. In fact, discovering what radio stations are being listened to by teens helps me understand the world in which the teens live. Knowing what types of music and groups a teen is interested in helps me to have a better grasp of who that person is. There are a number of resources that can help you "keep up" in this arena, such as the publication *Rolling Stone* and the cable TV network MTV.

If you enjoy movies, this may be a common area of interest that allows you to enter into the world of the teen you are trying to get to know. Books on various topics have all been successful common interests for adult workers with youth as they develop relationships with teens.

Many times a specific program or program emphasis can be developed from these common interests; for example, you may start a book club, a movie club, or a camp for bikers. Remember that as one creates or builds these programmatic areas of special interest, it is important to be faithful to your role as a Christian leader. A movie club that doesn't include conversation around the implications for the faith becomes just a movie club and not a ministry of the church.

The idea is to establish a common arena for conversation that adults and youth both enjoy so that trust and conversation can continue. School is always a possibility, although many teens think you are coming across as a parent when the topic of school comes up. By this I mean that the conversation can quickly shift to grades or how well teens are doing—parental interests. You may do better to focus more on teachers, life around school, or peer relationships than on academic achievement.

Find Time for the Teens

An important part of relationship building is finding the time to be with teens in informal or nonprogram settings. Certainly it is important to be around when programs and formal ministries are occurring, such as worship, but in developing relationships some of the most important times can be the informal periods.

- Do you stop by where teens work just to say hello?
- Do you know whether they are involved in activities and what those are? Even if you cannot show up where teens are active, you can make a point to ask them how it went the next time you see them.
- Do you make yourself available to them at appropriate times, such as arriving to program meetings early and staying late in case any of the teens want to talk?
- Do the teens know where you live or how to get in touch with you?
- Do you occasionally include them in your plans, such as taking a couple of them to the movies on Friday night?

If you don't spend time with teens and are not available for them, you will never develop a relationship with them. The most important part of congregational youth ministry, and the hardest to define, is the informal time you spend with them as relationships are developed and maintained.

Turf Issues

A significant way to build relationships with teens has been the willingness of adults to engage them on their "turf." This has different meanings for differing teens. In some situations this is as simple as being around at the teen's home or school. Indeed, a simple way to get to know a teen is to have lunch with her or him at the school cafeteria or to be around at school activities, such as athletic or band competitions. For others, their "turf" may be their workplace or a certain mall where they might gather.

For most churches located in suburbia or in rural areas, meeting teens on their "turf" is not a problem. In some cities, however, you must be careful about "turf" issues and how you are going to develop a relationship with these teens. Unfortunately, sometimes a teen's "turf" may well be a dangerous place for an outside adult. One must be careful about advocating a ministry of meeting teens on their "turf."

It is important to understand what a teen might call his or her "turf." Usually a teen's turf is where he or she ultimately feels at home and has some sense of belonging. It may be school, home, work, a mall, a parking lot, or a basketball court.

An Adult Friend, Not a Peer

A significant problem for youth ministry has been the number of adults who want so much to be accepted and liked by teens that they forget they are adults and can behave like teens. Youth ministry calls you to develop friendships and relationships with teens, but not to become one of them. You are an adult and as such the relationship you have with the teens must stay as an adult friend.

What relational ministry is all about is incarnating God to youth through your relationship as much as that is possible, given that you, like the teen, are human. It is about an adult taking the time to care for teens in a profoundly religious way. It is about adults who befriend youth on behalf of themselves, the church, and God.

All cultural groups have rites of passage, which signal the transition from childhood to adult responsibilities. In the United States cultural rites of passage that recognize the passage of children to teenagers and teenagers to adults have become diffused. Most teen groups have rites of passage that may or may not be identified as such. The issuing of a driver's license is an example of a significant rite of passage for many teens. For some, sexual activity has taken on the significance of an important rite of passage.

Relational youth ministry, in which adults of the church are engaged, will be informed by the rites of passage in the adolescent community in which the church finds itself. Adults ought to be willing to recognize the significance of these events in the life of each teen and be able to deal with these rites of passage in a theological manner. In those places where the rites of passage have antisocial or anti-Christian implications, the church will be pushed to develop other rites of passage and to invest these new ceremonies with as much significance as the cultural ones do in the lives of the adolescents they minister to/with/by.

The most neglected area of youth ministry over the past twenty years is relational ministry. Congregations need to develop and educate a cadre of adults who are willing to spend time and develop meaningful relationships with teens. This is even more important for the teens who reside in those places of our society that lack significant appropriate male models. We will now examine some of the aspects of developing and recruiting adults for this significant ministry.

As Jennifer, Betsy, and Dave reflected on building a relational ministry they realized that they had already begun the process. They all knew youth whom they talked with regularly. Now they had some sense of a plan about how to enrich those conversations and use them more effectively. They began to think of the questions they could ask that might help them gather useful information for programming and in getting to know the teens in their congregations youth ministry.

Of course, the relationship between the adults of the church and the youth are just one aspect of the relational ministry of the congregation. Youth need to be challenged to examine all the relationships of their life (such as with peers, God's creation, siblings, and parents) to make sure those relationships are a faithful reflection of their faith and belief.

TEN TOPICS TO EXPLORE WITH TEENS

Here are ten topics you might want to try to explore when talking with teens. These topics are designed to help you begin the process of developing a relationship with teenagers. The information you gather can be added to the index card (see above), if it is helpful. And it can be the basis for further conversation.

1. School
   Best and Worst Class and Teacher: _____
   Schedule: _____
2. Friends
   Who you hang with:_____
   What you do:_____
3. Music
   Latest CD you bought:_____
   Radio stations you listen to:_____
   Hottest new group:_____
   Latest concert you attended:_____
4. Films
   Last film you saw:_____
   Next film you want to see:_____
5. Television
   The shows you watch regularly:_____
   The shows you dislike:_____
6. Reading material
   Magazine you subscribe to:_____

    Type of books you like to read: _____

7. Outside Activities and Hobbies
Sports you participate in:_____
Sports you like to watch:_____
Other activities (such as camping):_____

8. Family
Brothers and sisters:_____
Do you share a bedroom?_____
Do you get along with parents, stepparent? Why or why not?_____
Favorite relative? Why?_____
Do you have chores at home? What are they?_____

9. Vacation
Favorite vacation:_____
Place you would really like to visit and why:
_____
Worse vacation_____:

10. Work
Do you work? Why or why not?_____
What do you do with the money you make?_____

CHAPTER 5

The Right Adults

Perhaps the most important part of youth ministry is the leadership that the congregation recruits to be a part of its youth ministry. Every church has members who do youth ministry without being recruited and many times without knowing they are involved in youth ministry. Chuck Kispaugh tells the story of a congregation in which the youth were asked to identify the leaders of their congregation's youth ministry. On all of the questionnaires was written the name of a very elderly man. It seems that he reads all of the local newspapers every day. If he found the name of a congregation member mentioned in an article, he cut out the article and gave it to the individual in church the following Sunday. This meant that he had contact with many of the young people, as he gave them newspaper articles about themselves. Through this simple activity, he established relationships with these young people, and showed them that the congregation, the people of God, cared about them. A simple thing, and yet a very important part of the congregation's youth ministry that most adults in the congregation did not even know was occurring.

I'm asked all the time about how to recruit adults for youth ministry. While there are no easy answers, one ought to start with a concept of the "type" of adult one wants to be involved in the congregation's youth ministry. There are several crucial gifts that adults ought to have if they are to be part of a congregation's youth ministry.

Having a Faith to Share

The most important qualification for ministry is faith. Adults who are going to be in ministry with youth need to have a faith that has some maturity to it and an ability to share that faith with others, especially with teenagers. Many churches find a young person or an enthusiastic couple to lead their youth ministry. There is nothing wrong with this, although many times the person(s) chosen has no real maturity in the faith. In fact, many times he or she is a very "young" and "immature" Christian. This person is still feeding on the milk of the faith, to use the apostle Paul's words. As these adults get to know the youth and develop relationships with them, important faith issues will be raised. Those young-in-the-faith leaders are placed in the position of being asked to help young people when they themselves have significant questions about their faith. Unfortunately, some of these young adults lack a wisdom that can be helpful in the teens' struggles with faith issues. All Christians struggle, at times, with their faith, and teenagers are no exception. Many of the adults recruited to work with the youth ministry don't have the maturity or life experience in the faith to help young people deal with the very complex issue of how one is a Christian in today's world.[1]

Churches in some traditions have frowned upon "sharing" the faith because it has been associated with gimmicks and tricks. To use another biblical image, churches have not wanted to be like so many "peddlers" of the faith. "Sharing the faith" is certainly more than the simplistic four spiritual laws or standing on a soapbox with a bull horn yelling "John 3:16" at everyone who leaves the football stadium.

As Christians, we are called to "share" our faith, especially when other people ask us about our faith. People asked John the Baptist what he was doing when he was baptizing in the river. He did not go to them. His faith and way of living were such that people asked him what he was about. Similarly, youth will ask their adult leaders about our faith, especially if we are living it. Unfortunately, many of us don't have any idea about how to talk about our faith. I am not referring to simplistic methodologies, but to a sharing of our faith stories in our own *words* and our own *images* that describe what our faith has meant to us. Thus adult workers with youth need to have a mature faith and some sense of how to share their faith with youth in their own words and images, in a language that makes sense to both the adult and the youth.

It is helpful to include how to share one's faith as a part of the process in educating the adults involved in the youth ministry of the congregation. This may involve having adults share with each other their faith stories until they are comfortable with telling of their faith journeys. At other times, it may take a more concentrated effort to help adults "share" about what God means to them, and how they live out their faith in their everyday life.

Another way to demonstrate how faith affects your life is to share a sense of the hope, joy, and excitement that are part of the Christian life and witness. We need adults who understand that the ultimate battle has been fought and that evil has been overcome. We need adults who have a faith to share, a faith that is alive, vibrant, and full of God's hope and promise for our lives and the world of God's creation.

Enjoying Young People

The adults who work with the congregation's ministry to/with/by young people must enjoy being with youth. This is not something that can be taught or learned. It is a gift that we have or we don't have. This gift can be refined and developed, but it cannot be taught. I have students who love visiting in a nursing home. They get energized by it. I have other students who can spend all day in a nursery and love every second of it. They get physically tired and perhaps even emotionally and spiritually drained, but they look forward to doing it again and again. Those in youth ministry must have the same feeling, the same gift, when it comes to dealing with youth. The adults ought to enjoy spending time and being with young people. Nothing is quite as deadly as having adults who know they are supposed to develop relationships with young people, but who really don't like young people or want to spend time with them.

Often, as I travel across the country and observe youth ministries, I see good ones and bad ones. One of the things I look for is what is happening in the informal or unplanned time. Are the adults off in a corner or another room by themselves or are they interacting with the youth? There is a world of difference between those programs and the relationships that develop between the youth and the adults when adults interact naturally with the youth and when the adults ignore or withdraw from the youth.

Those adults who enjoy young people have a deep respect and value for who youth are as persons. They are genuinely concerned about youth and are interested in the lives of young people. These adults have what I call "approachability." Teens seek them out. Young people believe these adults are approachable, and so youth are willing to enter into relationship with them. And finally these adults remember that they are adult friends of these youth and not youth themselves.

An Appropriate Sense of "Calling"

Leaders must have an appropriate sense of why they are involved in youth ministry. Too many times youth ministry has been virtually destroyed by adults who are in the ministry only to get their own needs met. While all of us have basic needs, and issues around relationships that we need to deal with in our lives, these cannot be so overwhelming that they take precedent over ministry to/with/by youth.

The field of youth ministry is full of stories of adults who have used youth or abused them, who have relived their wishes to be an adolescent athlete once again, or to be the most popular teen in town. There is no place in youth ministry for those whose personal needs are so great. These adults are still part of the church. They need Christian love, acceptance, and counseling, but they don't need to be placed in a position where their needs and conduct endanger the safety and wholeness of youth or the reputation of the ministry and church.

YOUR MOTIVATION FOR YOUTH MINISTRY

Here is a list of twenty-two reasons why people are involved in youth ministry. Identify the five reasons that correspond best with why you are now or want to be involved in youth ministry. Be honest with yourself!

_____ 1. The pastor was desperate.

_____ 2. I was made to feel guilty about not doing enough at the church.

_____ 3. I felt guilty that no one at the church cared enough to get involved.

_____ 4. I'm a parent of one of the youth, so I must serve my time.

_____ 5. I'm upset that the youth don't know the Bible.

_____ 6. I think the youth need to memorize scripture.

_____ 7. I want to make sure the youth have a personal relationship with God.

_____ 8. I want to make sure that the youth understand they ought to be working with God to make the world a better place.

_____ 9. I really don't like working with other adults.

_____10. I need to do something at the church.

_____11. I had a great adolescence and want the youth of today to have a great adolescence, too.

_____12. I had a miserable adolescence and want to make sure the youth of today don't have to experience what I went through.

_____13. I know that if only the youth of today would listen to me, everything would be all right in their world.

_____14. I enjoy working with young people and have had positive relationships with them in the past.

_____15. I feel God is calling me into this ministry.

_____16. I believe God wants me to be able to listen and hear young people today.

_____17. I want to be able to share what God has done in my life in a way that may be helpful to others.

_____18. I believe my skills and talents can be used in this ministry to serve others.

_____19. I want young people to feel good about themselves.

_____20. I want young people to have a vital faith that speaks to them in this day and age.

_____21. I was recruited by the youth miinistry team because they thought I had the gifts and skills they were looking for in the ministry.

_____22. I was recruited by several youth who thought I might be able to help them in their life as a Christian.

The first thirteen reasons listed tend to focus more on self, and the last nine reasons listed tend to focus on ministry to others. If your top four or five reasons for being involved in youth ministry are listed in the top thirteen statements, you may want to reexamine your motives for wanting to be in youth ministry.

"If we enter youth ministry for the purpose of getting our own needs met, there will come a point that our needs are destructive to the youth ministry." So states Larry Kefauver in *Starting a Youth Ministry*.[2] I believe he is right. Youth ministry is full of horror stories of adults involved in it for the wrong reasons. We must have adults working with youth for the right reasons: a sense of calling and commitment.

Time

Another key consideration in the type of adults you look for is the time they have available. Adults must have time to develop relationships with youth and to be involved in the other youth ministry experiences. Time is in short supply in our hectic world. The lifestyle that many of us have chosen to live is one full of activity. In fact, many of us, even those in the church, believe that by "doing" we can earn or increase our salvation. Nothing could be further from the truth. However, the feeling persists, and so we "do" activity after activity.

For an adult to be involved in youth ministry takes a major commitment of time. If the adults who are recruited do not have time for active involvement, then the ministry will suffer. Everywhere most youth turn, they find adults who are too busy to be with them and to spend time with them. This usually includes their parents as well as their teachers. The adults who are in youth ministry must have time to develop relationships and spend time with youth. This may mean *freeing these adults from other responsibilities at the church.*

If a church is really serious and committed to youth ministry, it will recruit adults to minister with/to/by youth and avoid putting those adults on other committees at the same time. If a church refrains from involving adult youth leaders in many other church responsibilities, these adults are more likely to have time to be with youth.

It is no accident that the most "successful" youth ministries have at least one or two adults who have been in place for a number of years. This doesn't mean that every adult has to make a commitment to a long-term ministry, but a few adults need to have some longevity. Too often youth ministries change adult leadership every nine months or every year. Thus teenagers may find themselves relating to six or seven different adults, one every year, during their adolescence. Deep relationships don't get maintained and sustained if the adults in the youth ministry are changing every nine months. Nor do parents or churches have the time to develop trust and support of a ministry that changes its leadership every year.

Yes, it is difficult to find and recruit adults who are willing to stay involved in youth ministry for a number of years. Yes, some adults start with the best intentions only to have circumstances change in their life, causing them to leave the ministry. But we must recognize, nonetheless, that it is best to have some adults with longevity involved in the ministry. The congregation needs to have adults who can carry forth the vision and the intentions of the youth ministry from year to year.

Listen

A key trait that many youth look for in adults is the willingness to listen to them. Our society has created a place where teens seem to be isolated from adults, with few adults who take the time to truly listen to teens. Instead teens are expected to always listen to adults. Many of those adults do not care about what the teens are thinking and feeling.

Unfortunately, this is true of many youth ministries. These ministries are full of adults who like to "preach" to youth—and I use the word *preach* in the most negative sense possible. These adults preach in a way in which there is no good news, there is no grace, and there is no hope. These adults seem to believe that they have something that they need to say to youth. They seem to believe that God has given them a special revelation and that they must tell youth what they need to know, hear, or believe or how to act in the world. They operate is if someone has given them permission to tell the youth exactly what life is all about, and they think that if youth would listen to them everything will be right with the world. In this type of ministry there is no dialogue, there is no mutual respect, there is no difference of opinion.

Youth need adults who are willing to listen to them. Youth need to have adults who are willing to hear their life stories and struggles. They need adults who don't make jokes about their lives and what gives them pain. Youth need adults who are able to get caught up in the rhythm of their lives. Many times, it is out of this listening that constructive programming that really meets the life issues of teens can be developed.

Nonjudgmental

Another trait that youth have identified as being important in the adults who are in ministry with/to/by them is the ability not only to listen but also to be nonjudgmental in their listening. This is, perhaps, one of the toughest traits to develop and learn. I know as a parent that if my teenage daughter told me she was pregnant, I would go through the roof. I would wonder how she could do this to herself and to our family, what about her future, and so on. I don't think I would put her out of the house, as Mary's parents seemed to do when she went off to visit Elizabeth in a far-off town (remember the Christmas story). However, I wouldn't be very happy with my daughter's behavior. Yet the ability to listen and not go through the roof is a trait that young people want in the adults who minister with/to/by them.

Many times youth will test you with a small issue to see how you will respond. Can you be trusted? Are you judgmental? Are you sympathetic? If teens find you can be trusted, are sympathetic, and are nonjudgmental in your attitude, then they may be ready to share with you what is really bothering them and what they are really wrestling with.

Being nonjudgmental does not mean accepting all of the behavior of youth. Nor does it mean not sharing your opinion with them, especially if they ask for that opinion. It may mean, however, suspending judgment for a time and helping them to deal with their feelings and with the situation. I am reminded always of the difference between love and like. The gospel calls us to love young people, to be concerned with their ultimate care and being. The gospel does not call us to like young people or always to be pleased with their actions. We can, as adults, show our love and still let it be known that we are not pleased with a particular behavior of the teen. This is difficult to be sure, yet a necessity nonetheless.

These traits are the kinds of things I look for in recruiting adults to youth ministry: a faith to share, enjoying young people, an appropriate sense of calling, available time, an ability to listen, and being nonjudgmental. Once we have found the adults to be in youth ministry we must remember to use their gifts and have adults who are willing to use their gifts.

Using the Gifts of Adult Volunteers

Sometimes we have the luxury of recruiting specific adults because of the gifts that they may have and the way those gifts will plug into the larger youth ministry of the congregation. At other times, the congregation's youth ministry does not have this luxury. We must use the gifts of those adults the congregation has recruited. It is inherently a mistake to ask adults or youth to try and do things that they cannot do.

It is important to know what gifts the adults bring to the ministry and find ways to utilize those gifts in the ministry. It is also important that the adults basically agree with and are willing to support the "intentions" of the youth ministry.

Is the adult generally in agreement with where the ministry is going and willing to be a part of getting the ministry to move in the same direction? In other words, the adults must agree to be a part of a team.

Different gifts of adults can fit into the different components of the congregation's youth ministry. Some adults are great teachers, others great listeners, some very creative and others good on follow-through. We can utilize all of these gifts in the appropriate places in the congregation's youth ministry. It is not helpful to have a great relational person who is poor at teaching, nor a great teacher who is uncomfortable in an informal setting trying to lead an informal youth fellowship meeting. It is not helpful to expect someone who isn't talented in music to develop a youth choir. We must utilize the gifts the adults bring in the appropriate place in the congregation's youth ministry.

Once we have a picture of the type of adults we are looking for and we realize that the congregation and the adults are willing to let the gifts and graces of the adults and congregation be used in youth ministry, we must recruit these individuals.

Recruitment

Recruitment is an ongoing task. It is never over. Those responsible for recruiting adults for the congregation's youth ministry must always be evaluating adults in the congregation for their gifts, not just for youth ministry but for the entire ministry of the congregation. Often when recruiting for one ministry program, one discovers that an adult's talent may fit into another portion of the congregation's ministry.

One recruitment tool is to provide potential leaders an opportunity to be involved in the congregation's youth ministry in a small way before they make a commitment to the ministry in a big way. That way, both the leaders of the youth ministry and the adults who are being asked to make a commitment have an opportunity to evaluate each other.

One of the most important recruitment tools for an effective youth ministry is to ask the youth in your church what adults they think would be helpful as leaders. A way of asking this question may be to determine which adults the youth particularly admire, look up to, or think are good role models in the congregation or even the community. Sometimes this method will produce names of adults whom the congregation never thought about as being appropriate youth leaders. Often the youth know more about which adults are in tune with them and can be of help in the congregational youth ministry than do the leaders. When recruiting these adults to become part of the youth ministry team, let them know that the youth are interested in their participation. This is often an important influence on their response.

Some churches may not have the luxury of being able to recruit different adults for the congregation's youth ministry. Many churches feel they are lucky if they can find a couple or one or two adults who will work in the youth ministry. But the reality is that if recruitment is ongoing, if we remember the umbrella concept of youth ministry, and if we include those adults who are building potential significant relationships with young people, most congregations will have more people than they realize involved in their youth ministry. Also, adults may be willing to be involved in youth ministry when they understand that they will be using the gifts they already have, and that they are only a part of the congregation's youth ministry. Many adults flee at the thought of being the person in charge of the entire youth fellowship program.

Educating the Adults

Educating the adults in the congregation's youth ministry is a crucial task that is often overlooked or ignored. At best, in many places, the adults are sent to a one-day workshop run by the denomination or a youth ministry outfit. A more systematic approach is needed. While each church and youth ministry is different, at least two issues in adult leadership education remain constant: helping adults discover, develop, and utilize their gifts; and having adults who support the intentions of the congregation's youth ministry.

Many adults are unfamiliar with what their gifts in ministry are. The concept of vocation or calling is sadly lacking in today's Christianity. Most denominations, while still holding forth a commitment to vocation, have produced little if any curricula or resources in the past twenty years to address this issue. Thus many adults have gone into a chosen profession, not because of some sense of vocation but because it brought prestige or money or it seemed like the thing to do.

God has blessed us with gifts, talents that God hopes we will use, and God calls us to use them. Many adults have no idea what their gifts are or how they can be used in ministry. The first task of educating adults is to help them understand what gifts they have and how these gifts can be used in ministry, especially in youth ministry.

Second, it is crucial to help the adults understand what the intentions of the congregation's youth ministry are all about. These adults may have even helped to shape or to refine these intentions. In any case, the adults need to be able to find intentions that they are in agreement with and are willing to support with their time, energy, gifts, and efforts.

A Brief Word for Larger Churches

For those of you who are ministering with/to/by youth in larger congregations where staff personnel have responsibility to the ministry, the staff can play a large part in the educating of adult leaders. I believe a helpful way to envision this is to think of the adults in the youth ministry as your youth ministry, as your youth so to speak. This means that the staff person becomes the head of the ministry and does a programmatic, relational, intentional, and faithful ministry to the adults who are in turn doing an intentional, faithful, programmatic, relational ministry to the youth.

Using this model, then, the staff personnel can plug in appropriate programmatic ministries that fit the local intention of youth ministry and the local needs of the adults. Obviously denominational training programs may be helpful, depending on the needs of the situation and the training being offered. Similarly the training offered by nondenominational youth ministries may be helpful, given the local setting.

J. David Stone's concept of the "Four Phases of Ease" can also be helpful in this type of education for adult leaders with youth. Stone's model calls for the "leader" to do the "event" (phase one) with the "volunteers" watching or participating; the leader to do the event with help from an adult "volunteer" (phase two); the adult volunteers to do the event with support from the leader (phase three); and the adult volunteers to do the event by themselves while the adult leader does something else (phase four).[3]

Keep three things in mind when you are using this helpful model. First, it can be shortened slightly. Many times one can skip phase one, having the adult volunteer work with the adult leader from the start. Second, this model can be used with youth as well as with adult leaders. So youth can be involved in this type of leadership training. Third, the adult or youth need to know that if you are the leader you are now doing some other form of ministry.

A Brief Word for Smaller Churches

Many of us who are involved in youth ministry do not have the luxury of a staff. Instead, a full- or part-time pastor has the responsibility of all types of ministry in the congregation. These pastors may be doing youth ministry themselves, or have recruited you to be involved in the youth ministry with them or with others or by yourself. Someone must take responsibility for your education and training. Often the only person who will take the responsibility is *you*. This means that you are going to have to begin to discover what your denomination is offering in the way of training and what else is available in your area for training in youth ministry.

A place to start is to call your denominational offices and discover what they have in your area. Another is to get on the mailing list of some of the nondenominational youth ministries. A third is to check with people in your area who are doing youth ministry. In most places of the country there is someone who is doing youth ministry full-time within an easy driving distance who will probably have a better idea of what is happening in the area and how you can get training. If all else fails, give me a call.

Educating Teens for Leadership

To be honest, this topic deserves another book. However, I want to mention briefly that this is an area that we need to be thinking about and working on in youth ministry.

Traditionally one of the ways we have educated youth to be leaders in the church and in our youth ministry is to teach them *Robert's Rules of Order,* help them to run a meeting, put them on some church committees or even denominational committees, perhaps even have them preach or help with worship. This methodology has broken down in many churches, and in many churches this methodology doesn't work anyway.

Part of the problem in developing teen leadership is the answer to the question What is a leader? How one answers that question determines how one will go about educating teens to be leaders. For example, many adult workers with youth believe that leadership is not an ability to run a meeting or to be involved with the administrative and decision-making aspect of a local church or a denomination, but rather leadership is expressed through some sort of moral living. Other adult workers with youth believe teen leadership is being involved in studying the Word, or simply showing up at every event and program that is offered by the church.

I do believe that developing teens who are leaders, helping teens develop the gifts for leadership that God may have given them, and sharing leadership with teens in the congregation's youth ministry ought to be one of the intentions of a congregation's youth ministry. Many churches seem to disagree with this assessment as they do nothing to develop teen leadership.

Burnout

One of the major problems in youth ministry, besides educating adult workers with youth, has been burnout. Many books have been written on this topic, and again a complete covering of this would entail another book. However, let us take a look at a couple of simple principles that may be useful in thinking about this issue.

Liking Youth

If the adults involved in youth ministry don't like youth or are doing this ministry out of some sense of guilt, or because no one else will do it, burnout will occur quickly. To avoid burnout one must avoid recruiting or using adults who really don't want to be involved in this ministry or who are involved simply because they feel guilty that no one is involved in the congregation's youth ministry. It is better to have no adults than to have adults who really aren't happy being a part of the youth ministry of the congregation.

Giving Support

Another frequent reason for adult burnout is that the adults don't feel that they receive adequate support. Remember, the issue here is the way the adults feel, not whether they actually are supported or not. Different people need differing levels of support. The adults involved in the congregation's youth ministry must feel as if the congregation is behind them and supports the ministry they are involved with. They want to feel wanted and know that what they are doing is important. They especially need to feel this support from the parents of the teens and from the leadership of the church, most specifically from the senior pastor.

Obviously there are many ways the adults can feel this support and many ways they can feel neglected—such as having their requests turned down by the local church's decision-making body. It is up to each congregation to develop a network of caring for those in ministry in general, youth ministry being no exception.[4]

Taking Time Off

Another issue in youth ministry that leads to burnout, especially in smaller congregations, is that the adults involved in youth ministry never feel as if they can get a break. In fact, if one is doing a good job with building relationships, this may happen often. However, all of us need a chance to take a break, to take a vacation, to breathe a deep breath. Thus some time off is very helpful. Again, people vary in their need for this, and one has to be sensitive to the needs of each adult.

Ongoing Faith Development

Often I have heard, "I'm tired of teaching; I want a chance to grow myself." Of course, I have also heard "I learn more by teaching than by being a student in a class." Our adult

77

workers with youth need an opportunity to grow in their faith. The adults, like the youth, need to be challenged and nurtured into developing the spiritual disciplines that speak to the rhythm of their lives and their faith journeys. For different people, the Christian disciplines that nurture and care for their being will be different—perhaps Bible study, perhaps a prayer fellowship, perhaps spiritual retreats, perhaps weekly or daily communion, perhaps an adult sharing group, perhaps ongoing work in a mission ministry. The ongoing faith development of adult workers with youth must not be neglected.

Having Realistic Intentions

One of the major differences between goals and objectives are that goals tend to be long term and objectives tend to be short term. An important part of an intentional ministry that can help prevent burnout is to have some intentions that are reachable quickly (objectives) as well as some intentions that are visions for the future (goals). If all our intentions are out of reach, people will become disillusioned and burn out. If, on the other hand, all our intentions are immediately achievable, the ministry will founder with a lack of long-term direction. Thus our intentions need to have some immediately achievable components as well as some long-term goals.

Asking for Help

The final tip I have for helping to head off or prevent burnout is to allow and enable the adults in the ministry to ask for help. Many times we give the impression that we as pastors or professionals are so busy that adults don't want to bother us with their seemingly petty concerns or problems. The adults allow a small issue to fester until it becomes a large problem and one that may lead to their disillusionment with the leadership of the church, the church itself, or the ministry of the congregation with/by/to youth. In giving the adult leadership the permission to ask for help and by checking with them often about whether they need help, many of these smaller issues can be resolved before they become problems.

The recruiting and educating of adults to be involved in the church's youth ministry is an ongoing task. It does not simply happen once a year. Adults need the opportunity to plug into the ministry at an incremental level they are happy with to explore whether this ministry is something they can truly use their gifts in and be involved with.

Educating adults, youth, and the congregation about the church's youth ministry is an ongoing task that involves a lot of thought and implementation. Each church needs to have someone who takes these responsibilities very seriously. In some smaller congregations it will be a volunteer or two, in other congregations the responsibility may rest with a staff person who can share it with others or personally take the responsibility. Whoever has this responsibility faces a difficult and awesome task. Many times the "effectiveness" of the congregation's youth ministry resides in his or her hands. Those persons need all of our support, help, and guidance.

CHAPTER 6

Choosing Topics and Developing Youth Ministry Programming

D ave, Jennifer, and Betsy were eager to understand how to build a "better" programmatic ministry in their congregation. They knew that a component of congregational youth ministry is program. However, too many people believe that the answer, or "secret," to their youth ministry is to find new and creative programming. They believe that if they can find the "best" program their youth ministry problems will be solved. Nothing could be further from the truth. Programming can aid an effective youth ministry, but youth ministry needs to be intentional, relational, and faithful as well as programmatic. Those who believe that program is the "secret" of youth ministry are in an endless search for the newest or latest program. They opt to buy all the latest "canned" programs or the latest material from their denominational headquarters or non-denominational publisher. They search endlessly to keep their cup of program filled from whatever well is available. Congregational youth ministry needs to pause and consider how to replenish the well that contains the water, instead of endlessly filling the program cup with whatever newest program is available.

We need to consider several issues in the building of appropriate and effective programming in congregational youth ministry. What follows is an attempt to have you look at how the well is constructed so that you can create your own well and not always depend on somebody else's "water."

Finding the Right Topics

There are at least four groups of people to be considered in the process of constructing the topics for programmatic congregational youth ministry: the congregational leaders and adult workers with youth, the youth themselves, the church (both locally and nationally, including parental concerns), and the wider youth community. The gifts, goals, needs, and objectives of each group should be taken into account in your planning. And every program should be "tested" against the standard of faithfulness—to the gospel and to the stated intentions of your ministry.

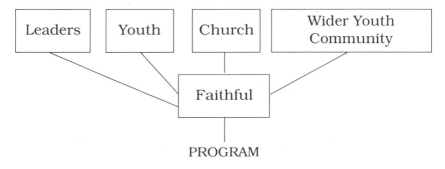

Leaders

Both youth and adult leaders are the start of programming. They know what they can and cannot do. They know the intentions of the ministry. They will direct the program-building process. Their gifts are the beginning of an effective programmatic youth ministry. Their ideas and concerns around topics for the programmatic youth ministry are important.

Youth

Topics youth want to explore in the congregation's ministry to them are also important, but we must remember the difference between wants and needs. Effective programmatic congregational youth ministry takes into account the needs of young people as well as the quality and ability of the leaders. Programs that do not meet the needs of young people will not get their support. And ultimately a youth ministry that meets only the wants of young people, rather than their needs, will die because of its superficiality and lack of relevance.

Relevance is a key issue for youth ministry. It is difficult to remain relevant. But one of the crucial issues of the gospel is for people to rise up in every generation and express the gospel message in the language and images of the day. One of the greatnesses of Paul is that he was able to express the gospel in the language and images of the people he met wherever he traveled.

Program that caters only to the wants of young people without exploring their needs in any depth will ultimately be irrelevant. We are to be faithful in our programming and our youth ministry. We are not merely an entertainment service, nor a babysitting service. While programs can be fun and entertaining, they must be faithful. We must help young people drink living water.

The difference between wants and needs can be perplexing one. One way of examining this issue is to ask whether the programs being suggested help youth put something back into the church and/or God's creation or simply take from the church and/or God's creation. If the program simply takes, it is probably a want rather than a need.'For example, a trip to an amusement park gives back nothing to the church, while serving a meal at church may give something to the congregation (fellowship), as well as allowing the youth an opportunity to raise money.

Complicating the issue between needs and wants is the fact that different Christians and Christian communities view the needs and wants of young people, indeed of all people, differently. Does everyone need a personal relationship with Christ to be fulfilled? Some Christians would answer yes; others would say that humankind needs a relationship with God, which may or may not be expressed through Christianity.

Several surveys that attempt to get out what youth want in youth ministry are available. Very few of these are able to make the distinction between wants and needs, or if they do, you are placed in the situation of having to trust the judgment of the makers of the survey. Still these surveys are a good place to start. I would recommend *Determining Needs in Your Youth Ministry*, by Peter Benson and Dorothy Williams (Loveland, Col.: Group Books, 1987).

So programming must be relevant to the lives of youth. The crucial issues for youth are different in differing communities and parts of the country. While some issues are the same across ethnic, socioeconomic, and lifestyle boundaries, some issues are particular to individual situations. There are many ways of discovering what the "crucial" issues are for the youth in your community. Developmentalists, such as Erik Erikson, Lawrence Kohlberg, and James Fowler, have helped us to understand these issues from their particular developmental perspectives. Others, such as Joan Lipsitz, David Elkind, and Joseph Kett, have brought the fields of history and sociology to bear in helping us understand the crucial issues for youth.[1] Many academic courses attempt to get at the crucial issues for youth by examining the work of these authors and others. Their contributions in helping us understand the "needs" of young people as well as their wants are profound and will continue to illumine us. Yet a program that is designed completely on theoretical knowledge can be stale and unimaginative. It can also hinder many adults from getting involved in youth ministry.

If one of the intentions of the congregation's youth ministry is to have youth actively involved in the planning, implementation, and evaluation processes of program development (and I believe it ought to be one of the intentions), it must be planned into the process. Youth can be active in program planning, in implementing the program, and in evaluating the program, but it takes time and effort. Having youth involved in all aspects of programming models a way of being in ministry that is participatory.

Nothing can help us understand the crucial issues for youth in a particular congregational setting better than simply listening to the stories, to the concerns, and to the rhythm of the life of the young people. It is precisely as the church, through its adults, enters into the world of adolescents by examining the work of theorists and by listening to youth themselves that the local congregation's youth ministry can discover the bonds of oppression that hold many young people captive and enslaved. It is these very bonds that need to be broken.

Church

Each local church is unique. It has unique needs as well as unique traditions that can be built upon and developed as program. Each local church has parents who have specific concerns and needs that ought to be an added ingredient in developing the topics for an effective programmatic youth ministry.

Besides the local church, many denominations have specific goals and concerns around youth ministry. These may be factored into the programmatic needs of the congregation's youth ministry. For example, some denominations are concerned with developing and fostering a sense of denominational identity, as well as Christian identity. This is a concern that can be addressed through the programmatic component of the congregation's youth ministry.

Some denominations have a well-developed confirmation program, and that is an important part of the youth ministry of the local church.

The concerns of the Church universal can also play a part as you begin to develop effective youth ministry programming. Is the ecumenical movement something that your church's youth ministry ought to be involved with? Do you want to focus on developing global citizens?

Wider Youth Community

Finally, consider the needs of those youth who are not directly involved in your church's ministry. This means making a careful study of the local as well as the universal situation in which youth today find themselves. No longer can the church ignore those youth who have not wandered in the door or been brought up in the church. Youth ministry, like any other form of ministry, has a missional, evangelistic, and social witness component. What are the needs of youth in the *community* in which you minister? What are the needs of youth in the wider global village that can be met in your congregation's programmatic youth ministry? Can your church host international youth for the school year? Can your church try to develop a ministry to/with/by youth in another community?

Youth ministry in every local setting must have effective program or content that is developed from the needs of its leadership, its young people, its church community, and from the wider youth community. Program, like all of youth ministry, must be faithful in its content.

If the programmatic content for your congregation's youth ministry:

- is built upon the goals and objectives of the youth ministry
- takes into account the leadership gifts of the adult workers with youth

- takes into account the leadership gifts of the youth themselves;
- is designed to meet the needs of young people in specific situations
- is designed to respond to the needs of specific churches within specific denominations
- and responds to the wider needs of youth—

THE PROGRAM AND CONTENT WILL BE EFFECTIVE.

Young people will respond favorably to this type of program. A program does not have to offer just fun and games to attract large numbers of young people, or have an external reward system in place to have young people attend programmatic youth ministry. Unfortunately, much of what passes for youth ministry does not take into account these four constituencies when designing the topics for programmatic youth ministry.

Some youth ministry focuses program strictly around the adult leadership. These forms of youth ministry develop an adult-centered program that includes only what the adults want to do. If the adult is dynamic, knows youth well, or is very entertaining, these forms of programmatic ministries flourish and grow. However, most of us aren't that entertaining, dynamic, or know youth that well. Besides being an inappropriate form of youth ministry (see the section on ministry with/to/by youth), these adult-centered programs are usually not broad enough to encompass all of the concerns that different youth may have in any particular local setting.

Other programs focus strictly on the needs of youth. Many times, these types of programs confuse the needs of young people with the wants of young people. Thus they develop programs that are based solely on what youth want to do. Few of us "want" to be called into serious discipleship or commitment. Most of us "want" to fall into the sin of sensuality.[2]

While some of these programs seem to be very effective, very rarely do they attempt to relate youth to the larger community, whether that be the local church community or the larger Christian community. Often these types of programs set up the church or parents as the outside force that needs to be overcome. These programs build group unity by focusing on a common enemy, which is usually identified as parents, the church, or the larger society. In other words, these types of programs run the danger of creating a community of youth and a few adults against the larger community, whether that be parents or the church institution.[3]

Still other youth ministry programs are concerned with "our" youth. These youth ministries seem to forget that there are other youth in the community and the larger world whom the gospel calls us to witness to. Evangelism or mission may be forgotten in these forms of programmatic ministry, or they may be understood strictly in a foreign context and not in our own neighborhoods.

Thus a well-conceived youth ministry program will take into account the needs of the leadership, the youth, the church community, both locally and nationally, including parents, and the wider youth community. It is as these "needs" are discovered or remembered and intentionally developed within the goals and objectives of the youth ministry that effective programs will be developed and implemented. Further, it is as these issues are explored that a church not only begins to "own" its youth ministry, but begins to see how all the parts of the youth ministry—Sunday school, worship, confirmation, youth fellowship, choir—come together and work for the glory of God.

A significant part of the planning process is allowing enough time for the program to be planned appropriately with the best resources available. Many excellent ideas founder for lack of time to pull off the concept. Some of the best youth ministry programs operate with at least a nine-month planning time.

Many people in youth ministry take exception to this type of advanced planning. They want not only to fly by the seat of their pants but to allow plenty of space for the work of the Holy Spirit. Yet this means many times programs do not happen due to lack of insightful planning, because people or curriculum or finances cannot be put into place due to a lack of time. The Holy Spirit can be involved in the planning process even nine months in advance!

The Program Pyramid

If you have been reading youth ministry material for any time at all, you have run across a helpful concept that I have adapted to my own use, and that I call the Program Pyramid. Essentially this concept says that one program cannot effectively reach all the different commitment levels and places young people are in their faith journeys. These levels are not always based on age or school grade. So various programs need to address the various levels of faith maturity of the young people in your youth ministry.

I usually talk about this pyramid and "levels" in this manner:

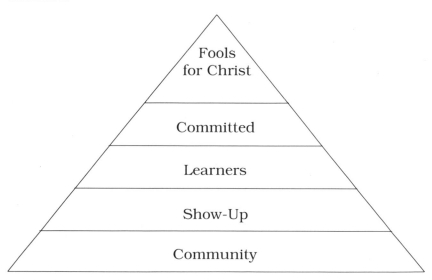

The largest number of young people in this program pyramid are community young people. This level includes anybody in the community who could possibly come or be involved in a program. Obviously not everybody comes, but the possibility is always there. Because this group includes everyone, you have a real variety of young people in various parts of their faith journey.

The next largest group is the young people who actually show up for any type of program. Again, these young people will probably have varying levels of commitment.

From this point on we want to begin to make a differentiation not in terms of numbers, although the numbers usually continue to decrease as we climb the pyramid, but on faith commitment or place in their faith journey. Any type of grouping begins to suggest that some youth are "better" than others. This is certainly not the case. However, in order to develop effective programs for all young people, some sense of their commitment level, their past and present knowledge, and their place in their own faith journey is helpful.

Thus the third level is those I call the learners. These young people have an active interest in learning. They may not always be regular in attendance at programs. They may not always express their interest to learn verbally. But they are willing and recognize the need for some program to have appropriate content. They are willing to have program delve into real life and what the Bible or their faith or their tradition may be saying about their life.

The next level are those who are "really" committed. These tend to be young people who are very active in many aspects of their youth ministry. They are willing and able to be leaders. They use good judgment and challenge themselves and their peers to keep growing in their faith.

The top level on this program pyramid are the "fools for Christ." These young people tend to be the exceptional young people, like Trevor Ferrell, who as an eleven-year-old started a ministry to the homeless in Philadelphia.[4] These young people, under the leadership of God's Spirit and God's church, have made an incredible difference in God's creation. These young people are wise in the faith beyond their years. Few of us may have the opportunity to learn and minister with these young people. However, they are around us, in our churches, and in our youth ministries.

What many youth ministries do in programming is design the program to meet the needs of only a portion of young people from the pyramid. Perhaps their youth ministry is focused only on the community or show-up type of young person. These programs call for little commitment and tend to continually introduce the church or the gospel to young people. On the other hand, some youth ministry programs are focused only on the committed and more highly committed young person.

Bill Wolfe, a past executive doing youth ministry in The United Methodist Church, has said that one of the problems for many young people who attend a youth ministry program for the first time is the language used in the church. He contends that these youth do not understand the language or the concepts that seem natural to us in the church. The youth don't know how to find the Gospel of John in the Bible. They don't understand what the Bible is or how to study it. These young people attend a program meeting for the first time and find themselves quickly "out of it" and, thinking themselves foolish, do not return.

Effective youth ministry needs to have programs that can focus on the various levels of the pyramid. Some programs ought to be focused on those who are more committed and ready to learn; others more on those young people who are still being introduced into the faith or being called to make a commitment to Christ. We make a mistake when we expect all of the youth to participate in all of the youth ministry programs. Youth need to be given the opportunity to join the youth ministry of your local congregation at the place where they are most ready. Then they need to be challenged to grow in their faith journey and to mature in their faith.

In some congregations the most committed young people tend to be peripherally involved in the youth ministry because there is little if anything that challenges them or calls for their commitment. In other congregations there is no way for those youth who are less committed or those youth who are from the community to find a place to start because the focus of the programmatic ministry is on the most mature young people.

Effective programming takes into account the different commitment levels of young people and provides programming for these differing levels. Effective programming is produced locally as a congregation creates its intentions for youth ministry. As the local congregation takes its intentions seriously it can begin to create effective programming. The local congregation is able to do this as it looks at its leadership and their gifts and potentials; the youth, their leadership, and their needs (as opposed to their wants); the church, including the desires of the parents and the denominational issues; and the wider youth community.

Many local congregations find that they are not equipped to completely create their own program. They turn to resources for their program. How to choose and go about this process is what we turn our attention to now.

CHAPTER 7

Resources
for Program

Imagine trying to produce a written resource that more than 39,000 local churches would find appropriate for their use. Differences in the intentions for youth ministry, in the understanding of what constitutes faithful Christian living, in ethnic makeup, in economic class, and in the size and location of a congregation all create different programmatic desires. All of these issues affect the type of written resources needed. Since many resources are written by a person or a group of persons having a specific situation in mind, one of the toughest problems for adult workers with youth is to find, adapt, or write their own resources. What I hope to do is give you some tips to remember in the process of using resources and help you take some control over what resource you and your congregation will use. First, some general remarks.

What Resources
Can and Cannot Do

Resources for programs in youth ministry include much more than just written pieces of curriculum. There are resources all around us that can be used, many of which are not written, such as people, audio resources, video resources, and places. So first think of resources in the larger sense and not in the sense of a written piece of curriculum.

What are the resources available in your community? In the town in which I live there are several camps, a college, a seminary, an observatory, several funeral homes, non-profit organizations such as Habitat for Humanity, lots of churches and pastors, just to name a few.

Resources can solve very few of your youth group or youth ministry problems. While most people are quick to blame the resource for creating the problem, most of the time there is another problem besides the resource. Many times there are serious issues at stake that are being ignored by simply saying, "I don't like the resource." A few of the more common issues at stake include: "I'm not happy with our tradition," especially prevalent where people church shop all the time; "I don't feel appreciated"; "I'm not getting enough support"; "I need help with behavioral problems"; the ministry or program is not relevant to the young people; the intentions of those complaining are not being met; those wanting a change have a theological problem with the tradition or resource. So people are quick to blame the resource instead of identifying the real problem.

Good resources are not a substitute for advance planning. Too much of youth programming is done at the last minute. While there is a place for the moving of the Holy Spirit and for changing plans to meet an immediate need (to be relevant), too much of youth ministry programming is done at the last minute in a hectic manner. A good planning tip is to be at least three months ahead in pulling program together and six to nine months ahead in planning the theme or topic.

Written resources must be used by someone. However, these resources are never a good substitute for a well-prepared, knowledgeable teacher, leader, or guide.

All resources have implied intentions and an implied theology. There is no such thing as a value-free resource. All resources have implied intentions about what the resource wants to have happen in youth ministry as well as an implied understanding of the faith. You would do well to ferret this intention out before using the resource, or have a time to debrief the youth and adults after the resource is used. For example, I make it a point to talk with the youth after any presentation by a speaker or organization, even if it is at camp.

Resources cannot cover up inadequate support from parents or the church. Parental and local church support are generally more helpful than all the resources in the world.

Resources must be used in an appropriate environment. The best resource in the world can be made ineffective by an inappropriate environment. For example, if you show a film at 2:00 P.M. with the sun coming through the windows and no way to block out the light, the quality of the film will be irrelevant. Or if you have senior highs sit in a circle on kindergarten chairs, the quality of your resource will not matter.

Thinking About Resources

People are the best and worst resource in the world. You need to know the gifts and graces of people who can help meet the intentional program needs of your youth ministry. These people can be members of your church or members of the larger community. An example might be the local funeral director helping with a unit on death and dying, or a missionary who talks with youth about her or his ministry in a foreign or home mission.

94

Places can be very helpful as well. Many times the environment can help to set a mood or develop a program. Think about the places that might be helpful in your youth ministry. Can you name some? Camps, retreat centers, museums, zoos, shelters for the homeless—all can aid in the programmatic part of youth ministry.

Many organizations have people who specialize in giving educational programs to teens on topics that will interest them. Some organizations have adults who are more than willing to include the religious component in their discussions if you request it. Many times these services are free or are available for a small donation.

The growing pool of audio and video resources is incredible. While I would never use a resource without first previewing it, you can find very helpful programs through denominational sources or through local libraries or through Christian education groups. These resources are usually inexpensive to rent.

After exhausting these possibilities, it may be time to turn your attention to written resources. Jennifer, Dave, and Betsy knew of the amazing variety of written resources available from a trip to their local Christian bookstore. They were a little uncertain about which resource would help them meet their intentions in youth ministry. You will have to make evaluations of written material. Are you ready to do so? Do you know how to evaluate a resource, whatever its format?

Evaluating Resources

I have included a lengthy list of questions that I ask whenever I am reviewing a resource. You must decide which of these questions, or what questions of your own, are most important for your program.

....

1. *Biblical Issues*

    •How does the resource treat biblical issues?

    _____

    •Which version of Scripture is used?

    _____

    •Does the resource use Scripture as a proof text or in a more responsible way?

    _____

....

2. *Theological Issues*

    •What theological issues are addressed by the resource? _____

    •Is the resource in harmony with the theology of your denomination or local church?

    _____

    •Are the theological issues raised appropriate for the age group involved?_____

    •Does the resource deal with youth in legalistic or graceful ways?_____

....

3. *Image of Church and/or Faith Community*

    •Does the resource have an image or understanding of the church?_____

    •Does the resource support the importance of the faith community? Does the resource believe that issues of faith are simply between the individual and God, that the church is not needed?

    _____

4. *Worship and Sacramental Understanding*

•Does the resource address sacramental issues?

_____

•Are those understandings in accord with the under-standing of your denomination or local church?

_____

•Does the resource address worship in any way? If so in what way?_____

5. *Educational Style and Learning Theory*

•What type of educational style is used by the re-source? Is it all lecture, discussion, or question and answer? _____

•Does the resource suggest action and then reflection?

_____

•Are the learners expected to simply receive informa-tion, or does the resource recognize that youth may have inherent knowledge that the resource helps them to discover?_____

6. *Cost Effectiveness and Availability*

•Is the resource reasonably priced?

_____

•Can you get the resource in a timely and reasonable manner? _____

....

7. *Assumptions About Teachers, Environment, and Learners*

   • What kind of time expectations does the resource have for teacher preparation? Will you spend that much time in preparation?_____

   • At what reading level must the leader and youth perform? Is that level appropriate for your youth?
   _____

   • Does the resource assume homework or preparation outside of the program for the learners? Will your youth get involved or committed enough to do homework? _____

   • What are the assumptions around the size of your youth group?_____

   • Can this resource be used in the environment in which you meet?_____

   • Do the lessons assume attendance at the previous week's lesson, or that the youth have some prior knowledge on the subject?
   _____

....

8. *Teacher/Learner Guide*

   • Is there a teacher/leader guide? If so, does the guide aid in teaching or providing background information?
   _____

   • Is there a separate piece for the youth? If so, is the youth material appropriate in pictures and words? Will your youth use the learners' guide?
   _____

....

9. *Environmental Issues*

   •Is the resource printed on recycled paper? Is there an excessive amount of packaging that will be thrown away?_____

10. *Overall Objectives or Intentions of the Resource*

    •What are the overall intentions of the resource? Are those intentions listed, or do you need to find them out? _____

    •Are the intentions compatible with the intentions of your congregation's youth ministry?

    _____

11. *Social Issues*

    •Does the resource address social issues? If so, from what perspective does the resource address those issues? _____

    •Are the statements in the resource in agreement with the denominational or local church understandings on those issues?_____

    •How will parents of your youth respond to these social issues being raised in the youth ministry?

    _____

12. *Up-to-Date and Relevant to Concerns of Your Youth*

    •Is the resource relevant to the life and concerns of the youth in your congregation's youth ministry?

    _____

•Are the pictures, languages, and phrases being used in touch with the life-style of the youth in your youth ministry and community?

_____

....

13. *Spiritual Growth*

•Does the resource provide for or encourage the spiritual growth of teens? If so, how does the resource expect youth to grow spiritually? Is that expectation in accord with your denomination's or local church's understanding of spiritual growth?

_____

....

14. *Denominationally Oriented*

•Is the resource denominationally produced? Does the resource hinder or help denominational understanding and loyalty?_____

....

15. *Image of God*

•What is the image of God presented by the resource?

_____

•Is the language used to describe God gender inclusive or strictly male or female?

_____

....

16. *Understanding of Human Beings*

•What is the understanding of human beings?

_____

•Does the resource assume that all people are sinful?

_____

•Does the resource address the issue of the goodness of creation?_____

•Does the resource show human beings in a way that they can change (i.e., repent)?

_____

....

17. *Is the Material User -Friendly*

•Can you follow the layout quickly and easily? Is the resource easy for you to use and to understand what you are supposed to do?

_____

....

18. *Inclusive or Exclusive—Diversity of the World*

•How does the resource picture people with handicapping conditions, of differing ethnic origin, of different gender, of different ages, of being single or married, of those with different socioeconomic status and lifestyles? Does the resource show a real, inclusive world or a narrow world view?

_____

....

19. *Packaging and Graphics*

•What kind of packaging and graphics are used?

_____

•Is the resource packaged attractively? Are the graphics and pictures up to date?

_____

•Will youth think the pictures are childish or too adult?_____

....

20. *Arts and Crafts, Music, and Drama*

•Does the resource use arts and crafts, music, or drama?_____

•Can an untrained teacher explain those activities?

_____

•Will youth respond to the activities suggested?

_____

Have I forgotten anything that you would use as a criterion for evaluating a resource? What things in this list would you stress?

....

I want to remind you that there are a tremendous variety of resources available. The problem is not finding resources, but knowing which resources are the most helpful, having the time and energy to locate the resources, and discovering how the resource ought to be used.

All of the large denominations publish their own resources. Each denomination operates with certain intentions and assumptions, and their criteria are different and change from time to time by the voting bodies of the denomination. It is a relatively simple matter to get a list of the criteria each denomination uses for guiding its written resource material, by writing the national office or by talking with those people who help to write and produce denominational material.

It is more difficult to get a handle on all the other resource materials that are not denominationally published. The youth field has seen an unbelievable explosion in resources available for youth ministry, from *Group* and Youth Specialities, the two largest nondenominational youth ministry specialists; to the branching out into youth fellowship material from publishers who previously published Sunday school-type resources, such as David C. Cook, Gospel Light, Scripture Press, and Standard Publishing. The success of Group and Youth Specialities has led not only to a large number of "youth" specialists offering written resources but the expansion of these nondenominational publishing ventures.

The publishing houses that are not connected to particular denominations tend to produce written resources with these common characteristics.

1. *Packaged very well:* These publishing ventures have had to make money over the years, so they have learned how to make their product attractive to buyers, which usually means bright, colorful pages with excellent graphics.
2. *Start with the Bible:* These materials almost always start with biblical material and rarely start with the life concerns of teenagers. The material assumes the authority of Scripture as the only means of understanding God's revelation in the world.
3. *Simplistic in theology and response to life's problems:* These materials tend to be very simplistic about the answers to very complex life situations and tend to have easy answers to very tough theological issues, such as salvation or revelation.
4. *Very practical:* The material tends to assume very little teacher knowledge and usually requires little teacher preparation time, especially in comparison to denominational material.
5. *User-friendly:* The material is usually very easy to use with teacher lessons laid out very well.
6. *Lack of ecclesiology and historical tradition:* Rarely does the material address ecclesiological or historical

issues; after all, this material must appeal to a wide audience, not just to specific denominations.

7. *Lack of liturgy and sacraments:* The material tends not to cover liturgical or sacramental issues, probably because of denominational differences.

8. *Sin and guilt:* The material usually focuses on sin and the need for forgiveness. Some have suggested this focus is overemphasized. Rarely, for example, would one find Matthew Fox's concern for the goodness of creation.[1]

9. *Authority:* The teacher is considered the authority with all the answers, not as a participant in the class, and Scripture is usually understood as the only way God is revealed, or the authority.

While many of the written resources from nondenominational publishing houses share the above characteristics, it is very difficult to create any kind of list of common characteristics for the plethora of material available for youth ministry. Take the time to examine the resource and then make an informed decision for yourself about whether it is appropriate for your congregation's youth ministry.

Jennifer, Dave, and Betsy could only nod their heads as this section of the workshop concluded. They knew from trips to the local Christian bookstore that everywhere, it seemed, was a written resource guaranteed to help their youth ministry. However, they were beginning to get a sense of what they were looking for in programmatic resources for youth ministry in their setting. The church and its leaders had been working hard at defining their intentions, and in understanding that each component of youth ministry had a limited function. They hoped that as their intentions became more specific and focused that choosing written resources would become easier.

They thought the evaluation criteria, while helpful, were too comprehensive to be of much use to them. They decided to list their own criteria based on their concerns and to evaluate other resources in the church based on this new evaluation tool.

CHAPTER 8

Working with Other Youth Ministry Organizations

What can be one of the more frustrating or rewarding aspects of youth ministry from a congregational perspective is relating to other organizations in the community that are attempting to "minister" (used in a general sense of the word) to youth. The agencies attempting to minister to youth in the larger community are extensive, and this book cannot even attempt to list them all. I do want to examine some of the organizations that you are more likely to come in contact with in your congregational youth ministry. I believe that cooperation is needed between many of the organizations serving youth, but some of the organizations serving youth may have goals and objectives that are either in direct conflict or dissimiliar with the goals and objectives of your local church's youth ministry.

Youth ministry from a congregational setting is never accomplished in a vacuum, but in a local community. Each local community has its own unique setting with its own set of problems and joys. Each community has differing organizations and agencies designed to support youth. Some of these organizations are unique to your local community. Other groups in your community are part of a much larger organization that may span the country or the globe.

The Juvenile Court System

The number and extent of crimes committed by youth in this country are staggering. According to one report, more crimes are committed in the United States by persons under twenty-five years old than by those over twenty-five. The statistics suggest that at least one out of every three youth will have a court date before they reach the age of eighteen.[1] Thus it is possible that members of your youth ministry may be involved in the juvenile court system.

Beginning in Cook County, Illinois, in 1899, a new concept began to take hold in the American judicial system. It was the concept that juvenile offenders ought to be treated differently than adult offenders. The court system in the United States began to believe that juvenile offenders, or wayward children, as they were thought of, were in need of protection and guidance. The court system believed that they should begin to emphasize treatment and rehabilitation and not punishment and retribution. The court's emphasis was on preventing the youth from performing a criminal act again. This concern and new way of viewing children in the court system was spurred by the growing child labor laws, compulsory school attendance laws, and the reform movements associated with each. These reforming movements had a lot of momentum, and by 1925 all the states in the union, except two, had in place a separate court system for juveniles.

The emphasis on treatment and prevention meant that over time rights that were prevalent in the adult court system, such as due process, rules of evidence, right to an attorney, and constitutional restraints, were ignored. It wasn't until the Supreme Court was forced to take action in 1967 that the juvenile court system, now firmly entrenched in the American legal process, began to give juveniles the basic rights that the adult judicial system are based on. The result of this Supreme Court decision and the criticisms of the system led to a reexamination and significant changes during the 1970s. The reforms led to what has been called the four D's:

> decriminalization, which simply reinforces the concept of treatment potential of young offenders; due process, by which basic human rights . . . are restored and which ensures that a young person who comes before the court will be treated fairly and will not be forgotten; deinstitutionalization, which demands the provision of alternatives to ineffective correctional facilities; and diversion, which attempts to place children in alternative services instead of facing the juvenile system.[2]

Currently the differences between the two court systems are breaking down. The juvenile court system has been forced to recognize most of the due process issues that are at work in the adult court system, and a significant and growing number of serious crimes are being committed by younger and younger youth. Both of these trends have led many prosecutors to begin to question the wisdom of a separate court system for juveniles, especially for serious offenders or the delinquent side of the court system. As the traditional methods of attempting to rehabilitate juvenile delinquents (jail and probation) have proven ineffective, new alternatives to treatment and prevention are being experimented with throughout the country.

The juvenile court system deals with three distinct types of issues: the victims of neglect or abuse; status offenders; and delinquents. Status offenders are those children and youth who commit acts that, if they were adults, would not be considered breaking the law. These activities account for between 25 and 40 percent of the juvenile court caseload. These acts include such things as running away, not going to school, drinking, and sexual promiscuity.

If you are going to be involved with youth ministry, in building relationships with young people, or in advocating on their behalf, you will run into youth who are in the court system. They may be in any part of the three segments. It will be helpful to have a basic knowledge of how your state and local juvenile systems work and how you can be in ministry with the young person involved in the court system for whatever reason. A visit to your juvenile court facility and conversation with judges or lawyers over how the system works in your community ought to help you minister more fully to the youth of your congregation and community.

The Scouting Movement

A significant ministry to youth in this country has been the Scouting movement. It has usually been connected with a the local church, but many of us in the local church have forgotten the Scouting movement as a viable ministry for the youth of our congregations.

In 1908, again as part of the social reform movements sweeping the old "British Empire," the concept of training boys in the essentials of good citizenship was started by Lieutenant General R. S. S. Baden-Powell. Originally designed for boys eleven to fourteen or fifteen years in age, this organization, whose mission was expressed in the book *Scouting for Boys,* caught on quickly and spread rapidly. In two short years the concept had spread to Chile, Canada, Australia, New Zealand, South Africa, Sweden, France, Norway, Mexico, Argentina, and the United States. By 1916, Wolf Cubs had been created in Great Britain for younger boys; this would be called the Cub Scouts in the United States. Eventually, older youth would be included through the addition of Explorers. By 1920, the first International Jamboree would be held, and the Scouting movement was underway.

Today the Boy Scouts of America have basic programs for boys ages six to fourteen, with Explorer Scouts (exploring career opportunities) and Varsity Scouts (high adventure) for high school students. Explorer Scouts are open to female membership, which stood about 40 percent in 1991.

Young girls were not left out of the Scouting movement. Following the pattern of the Boy Scouts, the Girl Guides was started in Great Britain. The concept was brought to the United States by Juliette Gordon Low in 1912 and became the Girl Scouts. Currently there are five divisions of Girl Scouts for girls ages five to seventeen: Daisies 5-6 years; Brownies 7-8 years; Junior Girl Scouts 9-11 years; Cadette Girl Scouts ages 12-14; Senior Girl Scouts ages 14-17. The purpose of this organization is to "inspire girls with the highest ideals of character, conduct, patriotism, and service that they may become happy and resourceful citizens" (preamble to the constitution of the Girl Scouts of the USA).

A similar organization, the Camp Fire Girls, was started by Dr. Luther Halsey Gulick and Charlotte Vetter Gulick in 1910. This organization has four divisions for girls ages seven through high school (Bluebirds, ages 7-8; Camp Fire Girls, ages 9-11; Junior High, ages 12-13; Horizon, ages 14-high school). The focus of this organization is on the concepts of work, health, and love. Several years ago this organization went coeducational, and in 1991 38 percent of its participants were male.

The Scouting movement has usually been connected with churches. Many of the lay leaders and pastoral leaders of churches were influential in the development and growth of the the movement in the United States. A majority of the Boy Scout troops meet in and are associated with a church. The Girl Scout movement and Camp Fire girls are not as connected to local churches as the Boy Scouts are, often choosing to meet in homes or at school facilities.

The United Methodist Church and the Church of Latter-Day Saints (Mormon) have led the way in the connection between the Scouting movement and churches. The United Methodist Church has more boys sponsored through its troops in Scouting than does any other organization. The Methodist Church as early as 1919 adopted Scouting as a midweek educational activity that could be considered part of the churches' educational program for youth.[3]

The Mormons have made the Scouting movement their official youth ministry. Thus each local "church" must have a troop. Additionally the Mormons are experimenting with their churches' paying all the fees for those youth involved in the Scouting movement sponsored by their churches.

While the United Methodists and the Mormons have been the denominations most directly involved, many other Protestant and Roman Catholic denominations in this country have been very supportive of the Scouting movement, especially the Presbyterian churches. A few denominations have tried to organize denominational groups based on the ideas of the Scouting movement.

There is a Commission for Church and Youth Agency Relationships. This Commission, essentially the Boy Scouts, the Girl Scouts, and the Camp Fire Girls, relates Protestant and Independent Christian churches to the Scouting movement. They publish a newsletter entitled *YouthScope*, which can be received by writing P.O. Box 6900, St. Louis, MO 63123.

If a Scout troop meets in your church building, someone in the church is acknowledging that the leaders and adults of the troop are appropriate people to be leading the organization. The acknowledgment is usually in the form of a document that someone in the church has signed, stating that the adults working with the Scouting program are of good moral character. The Boy Scout movement in particular is very eager to have support and connection between its members and the local church.

Here is a tremendous opportunity for ministry that we in many churches have overlooked in recent years. The possibility of evangelism is ripe. These young men and women in Scouting are looking for adult role models to help them build their future. What better place is there to be involved in the congregation's youth ministry?

Certainly the aspects of patriotism and the blending of God and country are problematic for some of us as Christians. However, the opportunity for ministry with these young men and women ought not to be overlooked or easily dismissed.

Independent Christian Youth Organizations

Over the past years significant ministries with young people have been established by Christians outside denominational boundaries. These groups may be alive and well in your community, or you may have never heard of these groups. These organizations may even be "competing" with your congregational-based youth ministry for the time and attention of "your" young people. These organizations and those who lead them may be working in concert with your church's youth ministry, or they may be hindering your church's youth ministry. The personalities involved at the local level will often determine the relationship and spirit of cooperation that may develop between your church's youth ministry and the ministry of these organizations.

This book makes no attempt to lift up all of these organizations but to address the more significant ones in terms of numbers of youth and adults involved and significance of their ministry in North America. You may have been a part of one of these groups when you were growing up or even today. You must decide, at a local level, how your church's ministry will be involved with these organizations. Some may welcome your help or cooperation. Others may have the idea that you are competing for the same youth. I have had both very positive and very negative experiences with many of these organizations as I've been involved in congregational youth ministry.

It must be remembered that these organizations, while they may have very fine goals, are not churches. They may have similar objectives to your congregation's youth ministry, but they are not the church. The five organizations that I examine are Young Life; Youth for Christ/International; InterVarsity Christian Fellowship of the USA; Fellowship of Christian Athletes; and Campus Crusade for Christ.

Young Life

In 1938, Jim Rayburn abandoned conventional church methods in an attempt to win a hearing from disinterested high school students. He began to hang out at school and places where youth congregate. In 1941, Rayburn, now a Presbyterian minister, and five others created Young Life as a ministry to high school students. Their express purpose was to proclaim in word and deed the Person and work of Jesus Christ to the adolescent community by any and every means as God directs. Their desire was for students to respond to Christ in a personal commitment of discipleship. To do this ministry, Young Life focuses on a particular high school. Their adults spend time at the school and establish weekly club meetings for students in various homes. Typically a club meeting involves singing, entertainment, and a brief Christian message. There is usually a smaller meeting each week, called Campaigners, for select youth that focuses on Bible study and personal discipleship growth. Young Life also has a large camping program.

The Young Life staff are responsible for raising their salaries and operating costs. They usually do this by donations from wealthy business people and whatever church contacts they have developed.

Young Life has developed a church model in which a church hires a Young Life trained and educated young adult, and the church pays that person's salary. This person has the responsibility of running the weekly club in a local high school and of running the church's youth ministry. This model has been well received in parts of Florida and Minnesota.

Campus Crusade for Christ, International

This organization was founded in 1951 by Bill and Vonette Bright at the UCLA campus. Its goal is to help fulfill the Great Commission. They attempt to do this by a multiplication theory ("each one reach one," and so on). The organization sees itself as an arm of the church in evangelism and discipleship. Its focus is mainly on college and university students, although it has ministries that work in a variety of areas, including prison ministry. This group also appears to be dependent upon church members for financial support. The organization primarily wants a person to say the words, "I accept Jesus Christ as my personal Lord and Savior."

Fellowship of Christian Athletes

In 1947, Presbyterian minister S. H. Shonefelt invited young student/coach Don McClannen to speak three minutes in his church on "Making Your Vocation Christian." From that invitation grew the organization known as the Fellowship of Christian Athletes, officially founded by Dr. Louis Evans, Jr. The purpose of the organization is to confront athletes and coaches with the challenge and adventure of following Christ and serving Christ through the fellowship of the church and their vocational choices.

High school chapters, or "Huddles," and college "Fellowships" are the basic ministry, with coaches being involved at various levels. Support opportunities for interested adults have been created, and the organization has been publishing a bimonthly magazine and newspaper.

InterVarsity Christian Fellowship

This organization grew out of the student movement in England in the 1870s. The deep concern for the spiritual needs of students by students led to local groups being formed on campuses. The movement reached the United States in the late 1930s and early 1940s. The group tends to focus on students and faculty members of colleges and universities, encouraging them to grow spiritually through prayer and study of the Bible. The fellowship is quite interested in publishing and has an extensive list of books, pamphlets, and a monthly magazine. This organization depends on church members for financial support.

Youth for Christ

This organization was founded in 1945 with a seven-point doctrinal program. It was an outgrowth of the Saturday night rallies that swept the country in the late 1930s and early 1940s. Billy Graham was its first full-time field worker. The organization has moved away from large weekly evangelical rallies and focuses now on Campus Life Clubs for high school students.

It has a ministry to young people involved in the legal system. This ministry, called Youth Guidance, focuses on youth in jails and youth homes, and operates with court referrals. Youth for Christ wants young people to understand and accept the person, work, and teachings of Jesus Christ. It publishes *Campus Life* magazine and a number of other resources.

One or more of these organizations may be active in your local community. Most of these organizations came about because those who founded them believed the church was not fulfilling part of its mission: to bring the message and love of Jesus Christ to young people. More often than not these perceptions were accurate. However, having all of these organizations in "competition" with congregational youth ministry is problematic. Hopefully, we can all work together toward similar, but not always the same, goals.

In your local community it would be helpful for you to be in contact with those independent youth-ministry focused organizations. Many of them have the expressed goal of getting young people connected to a local church after they have been "saved." Whether these organizations are able to do this is always a large question. In those communities where the local leaders take this goal seriously, your participation and help will generally be welcomed and applauded. In other places, the "competition" for the same young people to be in attendance and active will lead to less cooperative forms or possibilities of ministry.

It must be noted again that these organizations are not the church. While they may have laudable goals, they may approach youth ministry with differing objectives and goals than those of your congregation's youth ministry. At times, these organizations may stress loyalty to themselves over loyalty to a church or even Christ. Many of these organizations have a highly developed Christology while their understanding and communication of the doctrine of the Trinity is underdeveloped. The Old Testament is rarely discussed except to point toward Christ's coming. Most of these organizations have been slow to respond to women in positions of leadership. Many of the organizations have had significant trouble relating their "tactics" to urban youth and ethnic minority youth. They are usually much more successful with white, middle- to upper-middle-class youth in suburban settings. A few of these organizations are trying to tackle this issue head-on. Those efforts have not always been successful, but they are laudable.[4]

Youth Ministry Resourcing Groups

A significant number of youth ministry resourcing groups have arisen outside those sponsored or designed by denominational efforts. Many of these arose when denominations cut back on budget expenditures in the late 1960s. Two of these organizations are quite well known and have been in business for over twenty years. They are *Group* magazine and its spin-off endeavors, and Youth Specialties. These two organizations have created a very extensive and helpful network. They have gone from producing resources for adult workers to youth, to publishing youth ministry material, to working directly with youth. Many of us in congregational youth ministry use their resources, especially when it comes to youth groups. Not only have these two groups flourished, but also they have inspired a number of similar organizations all over the country. Some will be around for a while; others will quickly go out of business.

The ability of these groups to sell material and attract customers, who are usually local church people doing youth ministry, should point to the tremendous concern for youth ministry in the local congregation. Denominations have begun to take notice and are trying to respond to the needs of local congregations. However, the very mechanics of how large denominational structures create curriculum resources sometimes hinders denominational ability to respond and compete with these organizations. These organizations are usually centered on charismatic individuals who build up a body of disciples. Also, these organizations can respond very quickly to the changing youth climate, fads, and needs. Denominations tend to respond much less quickly in curriculum development and to shun developing programs around specific individuals and their talents.

Many local church leaders use the materials these organizations publish and sell without any sense of the objectives of the materials. Of course, many of these adults don't have a sense of what the objectives of their own youth ministry are either (see chapter 3). This leads to situations where the material being used is not in harmony with the implicit or explicit goals and objectives of the congregation's youth ministry. In the extreme case, the local church allows one of these group's material to set the goals and objectives for its congregational youth ministry. (Yes, local churches can also be guilty of allowing denominational resources to set their goals and objectives.)

I have used and will continue to use material from a tremendous variety of sources, including those I have discussed here. However, I use this material only when it supports previously established intentions (goals and objectives). Sometimes the material needs special handling or adaptation to fit the local youth ministry goals and objectives. Congregational youth ministry leaders need to be more particular and more careful about the material we use in our youth ministry and our youth groups.

Support Groups

A growing part of the North American culture is the self-help group. Any listing in a major newspaper shows an unbelievable array of these groups. The popularity of these groups has encouraged and enabled many of them to reach into the adolescent population. In the local community near where I live, there are self-help groups for teens who are from divorced situations; who have stepmoms or stepdads; whose parent(s) has been killed; who have been abused; who have a drinking problem (AlaTeen); who have a drug problem; or who have eating disorders. And the list might be longer in your community. Many of these groups have had successful ministries with young people. Some of the young people who are in the youth ministry of your congregation might need the specialized help these groups can provide, or they might already be involved in one or more of these groups.

The task of compiling a complete list of these organizations and their services is beyond the scope of this work. However, I encourage you to learn about the groups in your local community, especially if you have young people who might be candidates for the specialized ministry they can offer.

Interest Groups

Likewise, the number of interest groups that are available for teens is amazing. From athletics to music, each community has a wide cadre of available interest groups for teens to participate in. Some of these are offered through the schools or through adult organizations, such as Mothers Against Drunk Driving (MADD), or through community-based organizations, such as 4-H. The 4-H groups probably have more youth involved than any other youth serving agency in the country. They ask young people to focus on projects of their choice and to learn about food, nutrition, health, fitness, food preservation and preparation.

Often these interest groups compete with your ministry for the time, interest, and attention of the teens in your community. At times, your local church's ministry will "lose" teens to the specialized interests of these groups. Rather than bemoaning the growth of all of these groups, you may do well to see whether you can work with some of them. Often these groups are able to provide a special sense of self-worth and identity to teens who are desperately searching for some way to be unique, for some way to be recognized as special. While our theology affirms the uniqueness and specialness of each individual in God's creation, a special talent that can be developed by an interest group can help that knowledge become real and not an abstraction. Some major youth organizations include:

ASPIRA—supports Hispanic youth in the pursuit of education.

Big Brothers/Big Sisters of America—primarily a mentoring organization that provides same-sex role models for youth.

Boys and Girls Clubs of America—sponsors national sports programs and has at its core health and physical fitness goals.

119

COSSMHO—The National Coalition of Hispanic Health and Human Service Organizations, founded by community-based mental health professionals to improve services for Hispanics.

Future Homemakers of America—national vocational student organization, open to junior and senior high school students enrolled or previously enrolled in home economics. It focuses on youth-centered leadership and teaching leadership skills.

Girls Incorporated—offers a broad scope of activities in life management pertinent to girls.

National Network of Runaway and Youth Services—offers shelter and counseling to young people.

National Urban League—has some concerns with teens that tend to focus on pregnancy prevention and parenting skills, as well as drug concerns.

Outward Bound Schools—provide wilderness opportunities for youth 14 years and older to develop self-confidence, leadership skills, and the ability to work with others.

Rotary International, Interact Clubs—provides a youth organization designed to give young people the opportunity to work together in a world fellowship dedicated to service and international understanding.

Salvation Army—includes the Girls Guard and Adventure Corps, which focuses on health-related issues.

YMCA of the USA—focuses on building healthy minds, bodies, and spirits, usually through its physical facilities and related programs.

YWCA of the USA—creates opportunities for women's growth, leadership, and power.[5]

One of my students was pastoring a small church, fewer than 100 members, in a very rural county. He lamented that there was no youth ministry in his church. As we talked, I discovered that a very active 4-H group was meeting in his church. I asked him about this group, and he admitted he didn't know very much about it. The next week he excitedly told me that the 4-H group was led by some committed adults, all members of the church he was pastoring. He began to show up at the meetings, getting to know the youth and observe their projects. While there is still not a regular youth group meeting at the church, the pastor discovered a flourishing youth ministry right under his nose. Now he holds a youth gathering once a month, which attracts all the youth from the community, especially the 4-H'ers. The last time I heard from him, the monthly meeting was averaging over eighty in attendance.

We in the church have an opportunity to reach thousands of young people by networking and cooperating with agencies doing youth work in our communities. Don't let this opportunity escape your congregation's youth ministry. Work with the Scouts or the parachurch groups or the interest groups, if they are willing to work with you and your congregation's youth ministry. After all, the work is done for the glory of God, not just for us or our church.

CHAPTER 9

A Youth Fellowship Model

Jennifer, Dave, and Betsy decided that youth fellowship was going to be an intentional part of the ministry of their congregation. Now they wanted to organize and structure the youth fellowship. They had many options to choose from in the organization and structure of youth fellowship. You may decide to follow a model that your local church or denomination has outlined. Or you may decide to adapt their model to meet the specific intentions and programmatic concerns of your particular congregation. Or there may be a tradition at your local church of youth fellowship that may be worth exploring. I want to lay out a specific model for youth fellowship that I use and have found helpful. You may find this model helpful to use or to adapt to your local intentions.

The model I propose uses the same monthly model throughout the year. In this way, youth fellowship meets every week, usually four times a month. Although four times a year, there is a fifth meeting in the month.

The traditional youth fellowship meeting occurs on Sunday evening for about an hour or two. In some congregations evening worship immediately follows youth fellowship. This limits the time available for youth fellowship. However, the pattern of evening worship immediately following youth fellowship seems to be decreasing. While youth fellowships have usually met on Sunday, churches have found other meeting times helpful, including Saturday morning and any night of the week, from Sunday through Friday. Some youth fellowships have even begun to meet Sunday afternoon after morning worship. Depending on the intentions of your youth ministry and the local setting, you may want to explore another time besides the traditional Sunday evening.

In some places, youth fellowship has been held in conjunction with an evening meal. In this model, the meal comes either before or after the meeting time, often serving as a time when the junior high and senior high fellowships gather together. Thus the junior high youth fellowship might have its meeting and conclude with the meal; while the senior high group gathers at mealtime and then meets after the meal. Reasons behind this practice of having a meal include helping the parents by providing a meal for the teens involved; partipating in a time-honored tradition in which Christians break bread together; an "informal" time when adults and youth can engage in relational ministry; and the mealtime serves as a place where people can get to know "guests" or visitors.

Unfortunately, many of these reasons do not seem to work in actual practice in local congregations. Providing and coordinating the meals is often more hassle for the adults than providing a meal at home; the meal costs money, which teens would rather spend on fast food; some teens and their families don't have the money for the meal; the "informal" time quickly degenerates into a time of cliques and stressing the separateness of the group, not its community and cohesiveness; and many youth and adults simply take the mealtime as a time not to attend. However, having a meal does, in many places, hold the youth fellowship together, and you may want to explore whether you want to incorporate a meal into your youth fellowship model.

Fun and Fellowship

In my monthly model, one meeting each month is spent having Christian fun and developing Christian fellowship. It is my conviction that many of today's Christian teens have no idea how to enjoy themselves in a Christian manner. This meeting may involve excursions away from the church.

This may mean choosing to play specific games that your fellowship group has developed over time that they enjoy playing. Or it may mean developing simulation games, noncompetitive games, or trust-building games, specifically for your youth fellowship and for your specific intentions.

These fun and fellowship meetings can be a wonderful way to introduce your congregation to "community" and "show-up" level youth. These meetings can be a perfect time to begin the church's relational ministry to youth.

One must be careful not to always plan activities that cost money for this monthly meeting. It is very simple to fall into a pattern of playing putt-putt golf or bowling, always expensive. The leaders of the youth fellowship need to have some sense of the economic level of the youth who are attending. Scholarships, budget monies, and raising monies are all options for the youth who cannot afford to go on these outings. No one should be excluded from the youth ministry of the congregation because of his or her economic situation.

One must not assume that the rest of the meetings during the month will have neither fun nor fellowship. In fact, your intentions may be to build a real trusting fellowship in your youth fellowship part of youth ministry, thus you may spend much of your program time building and developing community and trust. However, the focus of this model is to have a specific meeting each month that focuses on fun and fellowship.

Missions/Service Projects

One youth fellowship meeting time a month ought to be devoted to missions/service. We Christians spend far too much time talking about our faith and far too little time acting on it. In many ways this missions/service emphasis is return to the mission orientation that youth fellowship groups had when they started in the late 1800s.

There are a lot of possible missions/service projects for youth fellowships. For some, this meeting time each month will be used to develop skills and to work on small projects that lead toward the summer's big service project. For other youth fellowships, this monthly meeting is a time to begin to explore what other Christians are doing in their local community in terms of missions/service and how your group can get involved. For example, soup kitchens, clothing banks, and local Habitat for Humanity chapters are all potential monthly missions/service projects.

Sadly, some congregational youth fellowships may need to start very tentatively as a tradition of missions/service may not be a part of their history. These groups may want to explore what projects they can be involved with that relate directly to the church, its property, and its members. It may be possible to introduce youth to those ministries that the congregation is already involved with and gradually build a tradition of missions/service.

Many youth fellowship groups get involved in mission projects at Thanksgiving, at Christmas, and perhaps even at Easter. Some may visit nursing homes, and others may have tremendous summer work camp experiences. It is my belief that we as Christians are called to be a witness in the world, year round. Youth fellowships should be involved in mission and service to the church and to the wider community, at least once a month.

Some adult workers with youth complain that they cannot find missions/service ministries for their youth to participate in. This may seem true at first glance, but a closer look at the community usually reveals a group of committed Christians working to make the community a better place to live, and reaching out to the poor and destitute. Additionally, most churches have members that really could use some help, even if that help is simply a weekly visit from one of the youth. For more mission/service project ideas, see *Beyond Leaf Raking: Learning to Serve/Serving to Learn* (Nashville: Abingdon Press, 1994).

The summer work camp model is one that can be expanded into a monthly concept. The summer work camp has developed into an incredible ministry in this country and abroad. If your youth have never participated in a summer work camp, they have missed a wonderful opportunity to learn of God and God's work in people and places around the country and the globe.

A significant part of the missions/service project ought to be "reflecting on the experience."[1] We have not always done a good job in helping youth understand why we as Christians are involved in missions/service projects or in helping the youth examine their feelings and their thoughts as they are involved in this type of ministry. This reflection part of the meeting is more difficult to plan and put together. Yet, reflection on our actions helps young people understand their faith from a biblical and theological perspective.[2]

Program

Two youth fellowship meetings a month ought to focus specifically on programmatic issues that have been identified (see chapter 6). While youth fellowship is just one part of a church's youth ministry, it needs program content as well as the fun and fellowship and missions/service components. During the meetings that concentrate on program, it is still possible and highly advantageous to spend a little bit of time on fun and fellowship issues. Play can help to break up the program structure as well as help to build community in the group.

We must also remember that worship or devotions is a part of every youth ministry experience. Devotions ought to be a part of every meeting, whether it is for fun and fellowship or for missions/service projects or for programs.

I prefer to have youth lead devotions, but many times youth are not ready for this leadership experience and need to be nurtured into leading worship. As the adult(s) models the leading of devotions, and as resources are provided for the youth, youth can begin to assume the responsibility for leading devotions.

Worship

In a month that has a fifth meeting time (four times a year), I spend that meeting focusing on worship. I believe Soren Kierkegaard's work can help us get a handle on the problem of worship in many of our churches.

Kierkegaard writes that most Christians believe that in worship they (the audience or congregation) ought to be entertained. The preacher, the choir, and the liturgists are understood as the entertainers. If God is present in this idea, then God serves as a prompter for those on stage, doing the entertaining. Part of the problem with this understanding of worship is that if you don't like the entertainment, you simply switch stations by going to another church or not attending. Kierkegaard believes that in correct worship, God is the audience and the congregation are the performers. The preacher, the choir, and the liturgist(s) serve only as the prompters. This concept places the responsibility for worship where it rightly belongs: on those in the congregation.[3]

I believe that Kierkegaard was on target with this illustration. Many youth appear to have no idea about worship, how to go about worshiping, or their responsibility in worship. So when a fifth meeting time occurs I focus that meeting on worship. Teaching about worship can take many forms, from visiting differing worship services, to developing worship services, to having a specific program where youth learn about parts of the worship service.

Many congregations have a tradition of a youth Sunday in which youth lead the congregation's worship. These fifth-Sunday meetings give one an opportunity to develop and focus on these "youth Sundays" without totally disrupting the programmatic ministry of youth fellowship.

A word on "youth Sundays": The youth need to be asked whether they want to be a part of this program. If they respond positively, then proceed; if not, then the congregation ought to rethink their options. Youth should not be forced to participate.

There are several ways to handle a "youth Sunday." The most common seems to have the adult advisor(s) plan the service and then get youth to "do" what the adults have already planned. This form is adult oriented. The four extra meeting times a year in the model I am suggesting provide an opportunity for youth to study worship. After this study, the youth will be able to develop and plan a worship service for the whole congregation and not just for youth or for the way the adult workers with youth want to worship.

Some congregations do not have a youth Sunday tradition, as youth are as much a part of worship as any other group. Youth have the opportunity to participate and lead worship throughout the year and not just one Sunday a year. I find this pattern preferable but difficult for many large congregations to develop or even understand.[4]

The model I have been describing is designed for adolescents who are usually found in high school. The following chapter will discuss groupings of adolescents for youth fellowship in more detail, but for the sake of this model one may want to adapt it to a younger or older population.

For an older population (for example, college students) the model would probably be just as effective.

For a younger population one might have an additional meeting devoted to fun and fellowship each month. On alternate months one could take the program meeting for extra fun and fellowship meeting from the programmatic meeting and on the other month take it from the missions/service project meeting. Younger teens need a larger amount of time spent on activity, developing community, and trust building. This age group doesn't always do well with verbal expressions, so active learning is to be preferred over verbal discussions.

Here, then, is a model that can be adapted for use in your local congregation's youth ministry. A diagram of this model might look something like this:

MONTHLY MODEL FOR
YOUTH FELLOWSHIP PROGRAMMING

Sunday ONE	Sunday TWO	Sunday THREE	Sunday FOUR	Sunday FIVE
Fun Fellowship	*Program*	*Mission Service*	*Program*	*Worship*

This diagram represents the youth fellowship part of the congregation's youth ministry. Most congregations have, in addition to the youth fellowship, both worship and Sunday school as part of their youth ministry. In keeping with our understanding of a comprehensive view of youth ministry, we could add other programs to meet the intentions of the congregation. For example, a congregation might add a Bible study or confirmation class, if that is part of the church's tradition; a movie or book club; camping ministry;

retreats; youth choir; handbell choirs; athletic team(s); parent and/or teen support group(s); prayer fellowship and/or study groups on various topics; and the like.

Two of these program areas, Bible study and retreats, require an additional word here. I have found a short period for Bible study to be the most successful in terms of involvement and commitment. I usually ask youth for a four- to eight-week commitment, in which they covenant together to attend every session. After that period has passed, we take a break and then start the Bible study again on another topic or biblical book. This short commitment period gives youth the opportunity to work the Bible study into their schedules. Youth also have the opportunity to commit to one study, and then not be involved in the next one, while other youth can then join the new study. Often youth feel, perhaps rightly so, that if they cannot attend for a few weeks, they will not know what is going on in the study once they return.

I favor two "spiritual" retreats a year for each grouping in the church. These retreats are not "lock-ins," which one of my colleagues has branded the work of the devil, because lock-ins too often have no real purpose but to allow the youth to stay up all night (which is not faithful and can be done at the home of one of the teens). These retreats are designed to further the spiritual growth of the participants, not to see how long they can stay up or how many video games they can play, or how many movies they can watch.

Each congregation must decide how its youth ministry will be designed. Most congregations desire some form of youth fellowship, in part because tradition has suggested that this is youth ministry. While congregations can have very effective youth ministries without youth fellowships, a youth fellowship group can have a very significant place in the youth ministry of a congregation.

The monthly model for youth fellowship meetings that I am suggesting has some of my assumptions around the intentions of youth ministry built into it. Can you name what some of those assumptions might be?

The emphasis on missions/service and worship show my own intentions, as does the suggestion that Bible study may best be done in another context of youth ministry—namely, a weekly Bible study. Your congregation may want to take my model and adapt it for your own use. You may want to incorporate some of the ideas contained within the model without using the model itself. You may want to use your local church's tradition or your denomination's tradition of youth fellowship meetings.

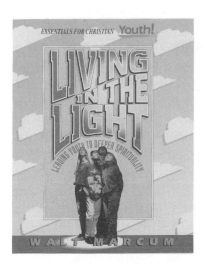

See *Living in the Light: Leading Youth to Deeper Spirituality* (Abingdon Press, 1994) for other ideas and information about worship, Bible study, and retreats.

CHAPTER 10

Making Youth Fellowship Work

One of the toughest issues in youth fellowship is how to group youth. Which youth should be a part of which group? How many youth fellowship groups? Each church will have to devise a plan for grouping for itself. For practical reasons, your church may want to echo the public school system in your area in its groupings pattern, as most of the youth who attend youth fellowship attend schools.

For the larger church, a pattern of grouping youth by grade level can be quite successful. Larger churches may have enough youth involved in fellowship to have *five* basic groups.

The first group is for those not yet in middle school or junior high but who have already begun puberty (see chapter 1). For these young people a weekly, ongoing youth fellowship may not be the most appropriate pattern. You may want a monthly meeting or a very intensive after-school program four or five days a week.

Some resource groups in youth ministry have already begun to produce materials to use with this particular group. Programming ought to emphasize activities and the building of relationships. The difference between boys and girls entering puberty is great, so leaders of these groups will be hard pressed to keep programs relevant, as the stage of physical and mental development can vary so greatly from individual to individual. It is important for these youngsters to be included in the youth ministry of the congregation. But it may not be appropriate to simply include them in whatever youth fellowship groups have been meeting. It may be more effective to form a separate group that can begin to develop not only its own program but its own tradition and identity as well.

Some of these youth fellowship groups for preteens who have started puberty meet during the week after school, as the crunch of school activities that occur in later years has not happened yet. Some churches have moved to an after school "youth club," where the youth meet every day after school, usually Monday through Thursday. Some places have gone to a monthly meeting or a bimonthly meeting instead of a weekly time together. Still others have simply expanded their Sunday school to include youth fellowship activities for this age group. These congregations have recognized the need to expand their ministry with these "new youth."

The second grouping is what has traditionally been called "junior high" youth fellowship. Because schooling patterns have become focused on available classroom space and class size in each district, rather than on educational theory, there is no longer a consistent definition of who attends junior highs or even middle schools today. Instead any configuration that can match available classroom space with numbers of students in any particular grade is used and developed. This makes it difficult to find a consistent "junior high" grouping, as it changes from community to community and even year to year within communities. Nonetheless this is a valuable age/grade grouping. Usually this group includes those young people in grades seven and eight, or ages twelve and thirteen. It may be better to keep classmates from school together rather than to keep strict age policies, as school is such a pervasive part of teen life. Classmates may share more in common, even if their respective ages are very different.

The traditional high school aged young person (grades nine to twelve) could form two different groups. The first group may focus on those entering high school (grades nine and ten)—the development of intimacy and identity, relationships with peers and parents, and the building of a really supportive community.

A fourth grouping is the second part of the "high school" group: those nearing completion of high school (grades eleven and twelve). Here the youth could begin to look at intimacy on a deeper level, saying good-bye to high school, separating from parents, the process of deciding a vocation and calling in life, and trying to develop a sense of what God wants each teen to do with his or her life, including college, career, and partner choices.

The last grouping would be for those who had graduated from high school or are older than eighteen and no longer in high school. In our society, once an individual has reached eighteen certain status and privileges are accorded him or her. Many are now working or going to colleges or to technical schools. These experiences are vastly different from high school. Yet these young people are still "youth" and need to be included in the youth ministry of a local congregation.

These groupings are suggestions for youth fellowship only, and not for all segments of your youth ministry. Sunday school classes usually parallel the school system, maintaining a consistent grade structure. Smaller churches, of course, often do not have separate classes for every grade. However, many larger churches need to have a strictly grade-level oriented Sunday school system. Other parts of the congregation's youth ministry may be able to include all the youth together, and others may need to find some other age grouping, such as over the age of sixteen for some athletic teams, or over thirteen for certain camps.

Smaller Churches

Many smaller churches have ignored groups one (the preteen) and five (post high school) and combined groups two through four. Usually this is done for one of two reasons: a lack of youth or a lack of adult workers with youth. While I sympathize with churches that have these problems, I encourage them to try to develop at least two separate groups. What normally happens in one large grouping is that individuals at either end of the spectrum feel the group is not for them and don't attend. In many places this means that once teens start working or get a driver's license they no longer are a part of youth fellowship. Essentially, in those churches youth fellowship functions for those younger than sixteen. This pattern is especially prevalent in churches where parents, feeling a need for preteen ministry (group one), lobby to have their preteens included in youth fellowship. Some churches are doing children's ministry and calling it youth fellowship.

In almost every case that I have observed or heard about, the thoughtful and careful separating of one larger youth fellowship group into two groups creates a larger total number of youth involved than before the separation. One strategy in separating the two groups is to allow those youth "on the borders" to decide which group they want to be a part of for that year. Then the following year the lines are completely delineated.

The vast majority of churches will probably have two youth fellowship groups. They may be under constant pressure to include the two groups who are still youth but not understood to be a part of youth fellowship: the preteen and the post-high school youth. One of the pressing issues for the church is how to respond in ministry with/to/by youth at either end of the spectrum.

135

Time of Meeting

The traditional time of youth fellowship meetings has been Sunday evening, perhaps with a meal (see the preceding chapter). While for many churches this traditional Sunday evening time continues to work best, I would encourage you to explore alternatives, especially if the Sunday evening or late afternoon time doesn't seem to be working. Downtown and inner-city churches have had a difficult time getting youth to attend youth fellowship on Sunday evening. Differing patterns have worked for different churches when exploring times other than Sunday evening for youth fellowship. Some churches have gone to meeting right after worship; others to Saturday morning; some to after high school sports events, usually Friday evening; and others to a week-night meeting. Whatever time seems most appropriate given your intentions and the nature and character of the youth and community in which you are in ministry ought to be explored.

Most states still have "release" time available for religious instruction. This means that with permission of parents and with a regular ongoing "class," the youth can be "released" from school, during school time, for "religious instruction." Not enough of us take advantage of this opportunity. It strikes me that this is a perfect way to deal with confirmation classes. So remember to be creative when thinking about time.

If we move this discussion beyond youth fellowship to other forms of youth ministry, we need to become creative about meeting times. I have found breakfast before school to be a very helpful time for Bible study and some small-group gatherings, such as prayer groups or relational meetings with one or two youth. Lunch times can be another meeting time either in the school cafeteria or at a local fast food place, depending on school attendance policies. You may need permission of school officials to visit on the school campus or parental permission for the students to meet you off campus during lunch.

Meeting Place

The meeting place for youth fellowship has tradition-ally been at the church. I have long advocated that youth need a place at the church to call their "own"—a place they can help shape and mold into what they want; a place that they can call their own and a place where the church can say, "Yes, these youth are ours!" Unfortunately, a pattern from the late 1960s and early 1970s developed where the place the youth could call their own was removed from where everyone else in the church gath-ered. This pattern was to convert an old house next to the church property into a type of youth annex to the church. While it was helpful that the youth had a place to call their own, the fact that it was a building disconnected from the main church structure gave the impression, usually correctly, that the rest of the church wanted little if anything to do with the youth of the congregation. Yes, youth need a place to call their own, but they also need the support and willingness of the congregation to accept them and ministry with/to/by them as an integral part of the congregation.

We must not limit our concept of meeting place to the church. Many smaller programs are finding great success in meeting in homes or in other environments than the church building. Again, one's intentions and the particu-lar nature of the group will have an effect on the choice of place.

You may want to consider using the spaces in which the others forms of youth ministry are gathering regu-larly. Perhaps the Bible study would be better held at someone's home or in the banquet room of a local restaurant for breakfast before school starts. The envi-ronment the group meets in will help to set the tone for that particular meeting, so choose the meeting space wisely.

Publicity

One of the most difficult, but crucial, parts of youth ministry and youth fellowship is publicity. How can you let people know where and when meetings or gatherings will take place? The most difficult part of meeting in different places at different times is getting the word out to the appropriate people, as well as letting potential first timers know of the meeting. Compounding this problem is the fact that communities sometimes have very different ways of sharing information. For example, in some communities letting a few teens know about an event ensures that the word will spread to everyone. In other communities, letting a few teens know will not mean a thing. In some rural communities or small family-dominated churches, telling a few key youth or adults will get the event publicized. In those communities where all the youth attend one high school, dropping by the high school may effectively get the word out about an event or a change of plans to most of the youth.

In some places, especially large suburban churches a much more systematic and formal means of communication is necessary. Ideas about how to do publicity in these settings abound. I have heard of churches using a call-in number that has a recorded message with up-to-date information about the youth program. This system works much like calling the movie theater about times for movies that are playing. Many churches have tried, with varying success, the "old" telephone tree, in which certain young people or adult workers with youth are responsible for calling members of the group. Unfortunately, no matter how telephone trees are structured, they seem to break down after a few months. Of course, you may decide to take it upon yourself to call everyone. This can work if you have a small number of youth involved, and call around dinner time, when many people are home.

These methods of publicity are especially useful for regular attenders of the youth fellowship program. These forms of publicity are not as helpful in reaching potential new attenders.

Larger programs must usually find other ways to publicize their events. A multifaceted approach is recommended:

1. *Bulletins* are a helpful place to start. This means, of course, that the event needs some advanced planning and that someone is responsible for getting the event placed in the bulletin.

2. *Announcements* from the pulpit are also helpful. This lets the youth know that their activities are important and helps to keep the whole church informed. However, both of these methods assume that the appropriate people are in worship, which we know is not always the case.

3. The *church newsletter* is another must in publicity. While these articles are helpful, not everyone reads or bothers to keep the church newsletter for easy reference. Church newsletters run the gamut from monthly, chatty newsletters to brief weekly newsletters.

4. A *prominent bulletin board* in the church is a logical channel for publicizing the congregation's youth ministry. The bulletin board can highlight past as well as upcoming events. It can serve as a way to recognize youth and adults as they minister.

5. *Regular postcards* can keep people informed of events and save the cost of first-class mail. This seems to work best in those suburban congregations where the young people are spread around the community.

6. *Visiting local schools* to hand out and post flyers is another helpful publicity technique. Of course, this won't reach every youth, but it can be helpful to keep the events before the youth.

7. *Don't forget the telephone.* Even if telephone calling systems break down, they can still be useful. Telephone calls are more personal than a postcard or a letter and often give you an opportunity to develop the relational ministry

of the church as well as to learn something more about the person on the other end of the telephone.

8. The *personal invitation* is still the most effective way to publicize events. While many times the specific information about an event is not remembered in a personal visit or with a personal invitation, the visit itself is most significant. A follow-up note can then be sent to confirm the particulars of the invitation.

Publicity and the Audience

This brings us to another significant problem with publicity: defining the audience to be addressed by the publicity. There are at least three audiences for any piece of youth publicity: the church, which wants to have a general idea of what is going on and some sense of how an event went; the parents or guardians of youth, who want the specific details, such as how much the activity will cost, permission slip deadlines, etc.; and the youth themselves, who are generally more interested in who else is going and what expectations will be placed on them if they go. It would be ideal to design each publicity piece for a specific audience. However, that may be beyond your resources, including budget and time. Still, you may want to fashion certain publicity pieces for specific audiences; for example, the announcement in the bulletin may be designed for the congregation as a whole, the letter to the parents, and the postcard as an excitement-building piece for the youth themselves.

Another helpful publicity tool is the youth newsletter. The most successful newsletters for youth are those designed, written, and produced by youth with help from adults. Many are erratic in schedule, coming out whenever the youth and adults have enough material and enough time and energy to produce the youth newsletter. While this type of newsletter is not always helpful for parents or for the dissemination of information about an upcoming event,

SAMPLE YOUTH
POSTCARD

YO! Dudes and Dudettes, the outrageous spiritual life retreat will be held at Camp Otterbein, October 3 and 4! Jamie, Cheryl, Jackie, Carl, and Jonie are already committed to going. To reserve your place, give this postcard to me, to the Bruders, or to someone from the church office.

BE THERE! ALOHA

SAMPLE CHURCH NEWSLETTER AND
BULLETIN ANNOUNCEMENT

ATTENTION! ATTENTION! The Ninth Annual Fall Spiritual Retreat for ninth and tenth graders will take place October 3 and 4 at Camp Otterbein. The Rev. Duffy James will be providing the program. For more information, contact Ed Dimmer or the Church Office. Let's all pray for the success of this retreat!

it can have a useful place in the congregation's youth ministry, especially in advocating for the voice of young people in the program and helping those in the program celebrate accomplishments.

SAMPLE LETTER TO THE PARENTS

August 30, 1994

Dear Parents:

The annual fall Spiritual Life Retreat for Mid-Highs (9th and 10th graders) will be held at Camp Otterbein (111-333-0000, emergency number), on October 3 and 4. The Bruders (Karl and Kris), Erica James, and Don Art will be chaperoning. Duffy James, the professor of evangelism from Nowhere Seminary, will be the speaker. Dr. James is an ordained UCC pastor and father of three teenagers.

The cost of the event is $10, which includes transportation, room, and board. The $10 fee must be paid to the church office by September 15. If we don't have on file in the church office a medical and parental consent form for your son or daughter for this year, please take care of this when you register your youth. A list of things for him or her to bring will be furnished at that time.

We will be leaving from the church parking lot at 9:00 A.M., Saturday morning, October 3, and plan to return to the church parking lot by 9:00 P.M. Sunday evening, October 4. Please let us know if we need to pick up or deliver your teen to another place besides the church.

Any questions? Give me a call or attend the fall parents' meeting, Monday, September 22, 7:00 P.M., in the church fellowship hall.

Yours in Christ,

Ed Dimmer

555-1000 (office)
555-2000 (home)

Budget and Finances

A perplexing problem for many youth fellowship and congregational youth ministries is the issue of budget and finances. Each denomination and individual church has different ideas on how stewardship fits into the life of the individual Christian and the life of the congregation.

For example, some churches do not believe in fund raisers. All monies for the church and its ministry are to be raised through the budget. In these cases, one must present a very organized and thorough budget request to the appropriate church committee up to a year and a half in advance. This calls for a high level of organization and structure in the budget request process for the congregation's youth ministry.

Other churches, while allowing for fund raisers, never want to have them in the church on Sunday. While not excluding fund raising, they set restrictions on where and how money is to be raised. They refer to Jesus and the moneychangers in the Temple, and state that they don't want to raise money on Sunday during worship. In these churches, careful planning must be done before any attempt to raise money for youth ministry is undertaken.

Other churches do not want any youth ministry money to come from the church budget. Rather, they believe the youth and interested parents ought to raise the entire youth ministry budget. This puts undue hardship on that program. What other part of the church's ministry has to raise its entire budget? Adult workers in these churches often experience burnout as they grow tired of raising money. I question the theological implication of asking youth to pay to be in mission with and for the congregation.

Some churches have established traditions where they have been able to raise significant sums of money for youth ministry. Many times through a single fund raiser, such as selling pumpkins at Thanksgiving or Christmas trees at Christmas, a church can raise its entire youth budget. I have seen examples of congregations raising over fifteen thousand dollars in this manner.

Still other churches operate without a budget structure. These churches spend money as God leads them, or as money is made available to them. In these churches, keeping the need and the vision of youth ministry before the congregation on a regular basis is a necessity.

However, most churches operate with a system of church-budgeted resources for youth ministry and fund raisers to supplement the budget. Traditionally salary and curriculum resources have come from the church budget, with money for programs such as fun/fellowship, work camp, and other ministries being raised outside of the budget process.

Choosing the fund raiser that works for you depends on many factors, including how much money you need to raise; how many youth and adults are willing to be involved; what other fund raisers are operating in your community; and the population you target, your church or the larger community. Many communities are overwhelmed with fund raisers from every group imaginable. If that is the case in your community, it may be time to emphasize the budget process rather than compete for limited fund-raising dollars. Parents of teens can feel this monetary stress in incredible ways when every organization their teen belongs to is trying to raise money, and they as parents are expected not only to contribute monetarily but to help in the fund-raising process as well.

In developing a budget for youth ministry to present to the budget-making committee of your congregation, emphasize how and where the money will be spent. It may be helpful to indicate how the money was spent the year before. Pictures and slides can be very effective in this process. The youth fellowship historian, whose function it is to record youth events with pictures and pertinent data for the records of the church, can be called upon to explain (sell) the budget to the congregation. Pictures help not only in publicity, advertising, and keeping tradition, but also in securing budgetary requests from official church boards and agencies. Many excellent youth ministries have been unrealized simply because leaders were unable to get the message (vision) across to the appropriate people in the church or larger community who held the purse strings.

I am one who favors spending the church's budgeted money on resources and programs designed to further the spiritual development of youth, such as camps and spiritual retreats, and not on fun/fellowship events. I believe the church ought to pay for all the resources needed for any aspect of the church's youth ministry—guest speakers, films, even magazine subscriptions for you to receive at home.

Knowing that the cost of fun and fellowship events can get out of hand, especially for families with lesser financial resources than others in the community, one ought always to be on the lookout for scholarship money. Many church groups, especially women's and men's fellowships, are willing to provide scholarships for youth to attend specific programs. You may also want to have a budgeted scholarship fund.

Certainly spending money for youth ministry is not in and of itself a way of judging a congregation's faithfulness. But it can be an indication of whether a congregation is serious about emphasizing and supporting its youth ministry.

Officers

Many youth fellowships operate without any type of elected officers. Other youth fellowships have myriad elected officials. Which is best for your youth fellowship depends once again on your intentions. A helpful rule of thumb is to determine whether the young people who are elected to office have an important function. If so, then you probably need to elect them; if not, why go through the charade of having officers?

The election of officers comes from a time when youth fellowships were run much like women's or men's organizations in a local church. The officers had specific functions and were held accountable to the tasks by the group. In many places, the specific functions that officers were needed for are no longer in place. In other youth fellowships, youth and adults refuse to hold officers accountable to their position and duties.

I have found several positions to be helpful in the way I have structured youth fellowship.

1. The *youth fellowship historian* keeps (and usually takes) photographs, videos, or written records of the events the youth fellowship (or youth ministry) participates in throughout the year. He or she also keeps files from past events. These records may have many uses, including being turned into slides to use to justify budget requests, used as gifts to outgoing seniors, or for publicity purposes.

2. A *treasurer* is also needed, if the adults and the church will allow youth to actually handle and deal with money matters. This is not a job for the parents of the youth who was elected treasurer. It is a position that ought to operate in conjunction with the adult in the youth fellowship who is handling and dealing with money and budget requests and disbursements.

3. *Publicity* may be the job that requires the most work. If you recall our discussion on publicity a few short pages ago, you realize the enormous task that may face a youth in coordinating and putting together the publicity. This job may mean everything from changing the bulletin board every week to writing the bulletin announcements or the youth article in the newsletter each week. Many times this job can be performed by two or three youth working in concert.

4. Most churches have *youth representatives* in the official governing structure of the church. Youth in these

positions need to be willing to advocate for youth, and they need to understand and appreciate the more formal process of making decisions. It is most helpful to elect youth to specific representative bodies rather than to simply send the "president" as the representative in all cases. And it can be helpful to assign an adult from each committee to work as a mentor with the youth representative, guiding the youth in the workings of the committee.

5. Selecting a *youth to serve on the program planning team* can create another helpful office. While some churches do planning as a total group; and others have just the adults do all the planning, I favor a mutual process where adults and youth join together in the planning process.[1]

6. As for *president* and *vice president*, you must determine what the function of each office is to be before electing youth to fill these roles. Most youth fellowships have gotten away from a business meeting model. I'm not convinced that that model of youth fellowship meetings is helpful in this day and age. So I would avoid having president and vice-president positions in youth fellowships.

Electing people to positions with clearly defined roles can help to alleviate the problem of turning the election into a popularity contest. Having midterm or yearly evaluations where the fellowship group evaluates the job performance of those elected can help individuals take responsibility for doing the jobs they were elected to do.

Business Meetings

As I said earlier, some youth fellowships include a business meeting that is conducted by the elected officers. In recent years, this type of meeting has fallen out of style, in part because there wasn't much business to conduct because adult workers with youth made the decisions, and because the combined junior high/senior high youth fellowships were not conducive to business meetings.

Other youth fellowships have been able to include business meetings. In these cases the meetings are run very efficiently by officers who have a clear agenda and with a youth fellowship group that understands business-meeting protocol—how to participate in a business meeting.

Whether your youth fellowship wants to have business meetings depends, once again, on your intentions. Most groups today deal informally with things that might have been covered in a business meeting, such as reports from planning committees or announcements about upcoming programs. If your group decides it wants to have a business meeting, the group and its officers must learn how to run business meetings quickly and efficiently.

Developing Youth Leaders

In times past, youth fellowships had a very clear role in developing youth to be leaders. Youth learned by participating in and by leading church meetings. Youth fellowships put a premium on helping youth learn how to run a meeting and teaching youth how to participate in large church situations where decisions were made. Part of the intentions of youth fellowships were to create youth leaders who were familiar with the church structure and how decisions were made, not only in the local church but in the national church as well. Youth participation was coveted by national denominational church groups, and so youth progressed from local to national leadership positions.

Today people have different perspectives on youth leaders. Some adults think a leader is one who affects the system from within; others think of moral leadership; others think of a leader as one whom other youth will agree to follow. The dynamics of youth leadership are much more complex than these three perspectives suggest, but they point to the problem.

Certainly, youth fellowships ought to develop youth to become leaders. But what is a leader? There is no consensus as to what real Christian leadership means, thus it is difficult to train youth to be leaders in the church. What are the characteristics of a leader? How does one "teach" them? As you answer those questions for your congregation, you can begin to focus on developing youth who are leaders in the church's youth fellowship program.

Youth Involved in Programming

In some congregations youth actually provide much of the programming, not only in terms of content but also in terms of leadership. In some churches this is limited to youth fellowships, while other churches allow young people to teach classes in the Christian education program.

If your congregation desires to have youth provide much of the programming (in other words, it is your intentions to have youth develop and lead the programmatic ministry), the youth must be given some training for this duty.

Evangelism
(or Increasing Your Attendance)

As Christians, we are called to share God's message with the world. In the church this has been called evangelism. Some churches confuse increasing attendance with evangelism. While evangelism may increase attendance, it does not necessarily have to, for the people you evangelize may go to another church or fit into the youth ministry of your congregation in another manner besides youth fellowship. Similarly, you may increase the attendance at youth fellowship without doing any evangelism.

If your goal is simply to increase attendance in youth fellowship, you probably need to concentrate on community and show-up types of programs. You will need to make increased attendance one of your main intentions and work toward that goal, rather than simply talk about it and go about business as usual.

A former student of mine was hired to increase the attendance of a youth fellowship and did so rather quickly. In four months the attendance had doubled and then doubled again, but the congregation was unhappy. It seems that none of the new attenders were members of the church or connected in any way to the church. The meetings were taking place not on Sunday night, but on Wednesday night. The meetings were in the homes of these newly recruited young people. So before you attempt to increase attendance at youth fellowship, be sure to clarify your intentions or the intentions of the church. Why do you want more youth in this part of your youth ministry? Are you ready to change what you have been doing in youth fellowship to bring in new members?

Another former student of mine was interviewing at a church who wanted her to minister to youth full time. The adults wanted youth fellowship attendance to increase. She attended two youth fellowship meetings and quickly surmised that one of the reasons why the numbers were so low was that the programs were not meeting the needs of youth, and so many youth had stopped attending. Now for the five youth who were attending the fellowship, the meetings were perfect, and they did not want them to change. So while the adults wanted the numbers to increase in youth fellowship, the youth wanted their fellowship to stay exactly the way it was.

Sometimes congregations forget that in having youth who are active in a "failing" program, the church is not listening to the youth who have chosen not to be a part of this program, or who may have a totally different perspective from those youth who are active. I've seen this many times in denominational youth gatherings. The youth who are elected to serve on committees and church structures that determine the direction of the denomination's youth ministry are the very ones who have an investment in keeping the youth ministry the same as it always has been, for that is what these youth know and what has ministered to them. Those youth who haven't been served by the denomination's youth ministry are not in a position to be elected to any of the offices or positions that could change the denomination's youth ministry.

How might one increase attendance? One strategy would be to divide the group in two, as this usually produces immediate growth of a couple of people, especially if the original group is a combined junior high/senior high fellowship. Another strategy might be to assign every youth and adult two persons you have identified who might want to become part of the church's youth fellowship. These persons would make at least two weekly contacts with the prospective member on an ongoing basis. In the terms we have been using, the youth and adults already attending youth fellowship would develop a personal relationship with these people who are not attending and continually invite them to community and show-up level programming. Another strategy would be to ask several adults to commit to spending their free time at the local high school, getting to know youth, developing relationships with them, and inviting them to meetings. One strategy that I would not recommend (because I am not convinced it is faithful), but that has been "successful," is to create all kinds of contests with prizes. I am familiar with a church that began to have contests that gave away CD players, $100 cash, and other expensive awards to increase attendance. The attendance in the program climbed quickly as the word spread about these "prizes." I encourage you to measure your methods against a standard of faithfulness you have set with the help of your congregation.

A significant issue to remember is that it is easier to get people to start attending in August and September, the start of school, than it is in February. Also, it is often easier to get people who are not members of your church to attend, as they do not have negative experiences that must be overcome.

If you are really interested in evangelism and not just in increasing attendance, most of your denomination's evangelism programs can easily be adapted to a youth population. If evangelism is truly your goal, you may need to help young people feel comfortable with talking about their faith. Youth will listen to other youth, who can talk in their own language about what the faith has meant and means to them. As youth are better able to express their faith in their own words, and as they attempt to live out their faith in their community, evangelism becomes much more a reality in the local community.

Jennifer, Dave, and Betsy knew they faced a lot of issues in creating and dealing with their youth fellowship, but they also had a sense that they were on the right path. They looked over their notes and decided that they were ready to start a youth fellowship group.

CHAPTER 11

Ten Common Mistakes in Youth Ministry

Based on everything they had heard, Betsy, Dave, and Jennifer created a list of ten of the most common mistakes in youth ministry.

1. Unclear Definition of *Youth*

A very fuzzy definition of *youth* is a problem for many youth ministries. Should the youth ministry include ten-year-olds or nineteen-year-olds or sixth graders or those who have graduated from high school? These questions do not have absolute answers, but the answers your church provides are helpful in guiding the adult leaders of youth. For a youth ministry to be "successful" it needs to have some sense of the population it is serving. The congregation may opt not to have younger youth (ages 10-12) or older youth (after age 18) in youth fellowship, but the congregation must include these two age groups in their own ministry.

2. Mistaking Youth Fellowship for Youth Ministry

Youth ministry is not just youth fellowship. The umbrella concept of youth ministry must be remembered. No one part of the youth ministry of a congregation can meet everyone's expectations. Similarly, no one program can do everything that ought to be done in a congregation's ministry with/to/by youth. No matter how small or large your church, youth fellowship is just a part of the congregation's youth ministry.

3. Thinking That Youth Ministry Is Just Program

A third common mistake is to understand youth ministry as simply program. There is little, if any, contact or relational ministry. The focus of the ministry is always on content. The adults and youth have no contact outside of the youth ministry meeting time. Adults don't build relationships with young people.

This misunderstanding occurs in large churches as well as in small ones. In fact, many large churches suffer from this when paid professional staff understand their position in terms of creating and preparing program and not in a more holistic understanding of being involved in ministry. Many times the patient, sustaining gift of presence is given up for another program.

4. Forgetting the Family and School Focus

Another common mistake is to forget that for the majority of young people life is controlled by family and school. It is imperative to know what is going on in both spheres of a young person's life. At times, the adult workers with youth may know what is going on in the family, but they don't know what is going on at the school. Often those fellowships that do place an emphasis on the school forget the home environment and have no idea what is going on at home. It is important to know what is going on at school, to have contact with school officials, and to have contact with the parents. One would do well to visit in the school and in the home.

5. Recruiting the Wrong Volunteers

Another error is allowing inappropriate adults to volunteer in the youth ministry. Too often the request for adults to work with youth comes as a blanket invitation to any warm body. While recruiting adults is often difficult, many churches would be better off without a youth fellowship than with the wrong adults leading the ministry. The church needs to maintain oversight of adults working with/to/by young people. This does not mean that we need perfect adults or adults who cannot make mistakes or grow in their ability to be a part of a congregation's youth ministry, but it does mean that we need to carefully consider the gifts and graces of all those who will be in direct contact with the young people of each congregation.

6. Ignoring the Older Youth

In a congregation's desire to build a successful youth fellowship or even youth ministry, the older youth may be sacrificed so that the youth fellowship can be built around younger youth. These younger youth will potentially follow the program through the years they are in the congregation. While this option seems to be sensible, often what occurs is that the youth fellowship gains a reputation as appropriate only for younger teens. The unwritten understanding is that when a young person reaches sixteen, gets a driver's license, or assumes part-time work, he or she leaves youth fellowship. While it is helpful, at times, to build a youth fellowship with younger youth, one cannot forget or give up on older youth. Youth ministry must be comprehensive to all youth, and it is a mistake to ignore those of a certain age.

7. Not Allowing Youth to Lead

Another common mistake is not taking youth and their leadership abilities seriously. Too many youth fellowships are run by adults. These adult youth leaders forget that good ministry is with youth and by youth. A good youth ministry needs to take youth seriously, listening to their voice, perhaps even giving youth a voice (advocating). While it is often difficult for those adults who are in leadership positions in youth ministry to have their ideas questioned, youth need the opportunity to speak, to disagree, and to form and implement their own ideas. A successful youth fellowship will devise a way to develop youth as leaders in their fellowship.

8. Being Too Tied to Tradition

Don't be afraid to try new ideas, attempt new programs, develop new traditions, and challenge old traditions. In youth ministry, as well as youth fellowship, traditions become established in two or three years. Some are helpful; others need to be challenged or done away with. We cannot be too tied to the past in our youth ministry. Every three or four years, not only do the young people change, but the community and world in which the young people are growing up in changes as well. Rigidity of program and being too tied to the past make up another common mistake in youth fellowship.

9. Overemphasizing Entertainment

Sometimes youth fellowships are created by congregations to be merely a babysitting group. In these situations, youth fellowship avoids any serious grappling with issues of faith, especially as those faith issues affect our world at large. A faithful youth ministry will not avoid serious social concerns. Being a Christian is a serious matter, and what

God expects and wants of us is a serious issue. None of us has the definitive answer to what God desires of us, but we must help youth struggle with their questions of faith and their response in this world at this time.

10. Ignoring Youth's Hunger for the Holy

Youth have a hunger for the holy. While many youth will not admit or perhaps even acknowledge this hunger, it exists nonetheless (just as it exists in the lives of adults in God's creation). Youth ministry needs to help youth understand this hunger, deal with the hunger, and celebrate God's sometimes mysterious presence in the world. Unfortunately, few congregations deal with this hunger in any substantial way.

Conclusion

If you are in youth ministry for any length of time, you will discover that it is much like any other form of ministry. Youth ministry starts with youth, but it quickly spreads into a holistic understanding of ministry. Being concerned with youth means being concerned with their family situation, including parents and siblings. Being concerned with youth means being concerned about the cultural and socictal norms that shape the institutions, both familial and societal, that youth participate in and live in. Being concerned with youth means being willing to advocate on their behalf. Being concerned with youth means listening to the voices of youth who are often unheard by adults in this culture. Being concerned with youth means being concerned with all of God's creation. Youth ministry, like any other form of ministry, leads us into concern for the whole situation in which human beings find themselves.

We have reached the end of the discussion about youth ministry for now. One of the impressions many students get after leaving my classes is that they must be doing a

poor job of youth ministry. They haven't been doing anything like what I've been describing in the preceding pages.
They feel unworthy and unappreciated. They begin to question whether they have gifts and graces and ought to be
involved in youth ministry. One of the problems with anyone's talking about youth ministry is that we tend to focus
on our successes and not on our failures. We talk about all
those great things we or others are doing in youth ministry
and fail to notice the mundane things that keep the ministry
alive in countless congregations. We don't share all of our
mistakes, trials, and tribulations. I want to assure you that
we all have those moments when, despite our best-laid
plans and intentions, things fall apart.

This handbook is meant only to start the conversation
about your congregation's youth ministry. It is not the
"Bible" for youth ministry. No one has all the answers in
youth ministry. I have attempted to share with you, in a
simple, straightforward manner, what I believe about youth
ministry and how I think you can help youth ministry
happen in your congregation.

We must walk a fine line in our theological understanding of youth ministry between arrogant pride and not
responding to God's ordinances. Too many times the youth
ministry lives or dies with the adult leaders. This might lead
us to think that the ministry is "our" ministry, not the
ministry of God and the church. Our hope is placed on
human abilities and knowledge. We begin to believe that
using this technique or that strategy can make youth
ministry work. This is simply not the case. We are not God,
and God's Spirit refuses to be limited by us and our failings.

On the other hand, there are people who believe that God
always operates in human history miraculously. They expect God to break into their congregation and divinely fix
the youth ministry. While I affirm that God has this power,
I also note that God rarely uses power in this way. Rather,
God allows us creatures to become involved in the process
of creation and life with God.

If a congregation is to have a successful youth ministry, it will happen because the people of God, using the gifts and graces given to them by God, have joined with God's Spirit and with the young people. Youth ministry takes both prayer and action.

This handbook cannot guarantee success in youth ministry. However, if a congregation follows the principles developed here, then with the leading of God's Spirit, I believe an appropriate youth ministry for that congregation will be developed.

Grace and peace in your efforts and in your ministry with God. God bless!

NOTES

1. Rethinking Youth Ministry

1. See J. M. Tanner, "Sequence, Tempo, and Individual Variation in the Growth and Development of Boys and Girls Aged Twelve to Sixteen," in R. E. Grinder, ed., *Studies in Adolescence* (New York, Macmillan, 1975), 502-22.
2. David Elkind, *All Grown Up and No Place to Go: Teenagers in Crisis* (Reading, Mass.: Addison-Wesley, 1984).
3. *Carnegie Quarterly* 35, 1 and 2 (Winter/Spring 1990): 1.
4. See David Watson, *God Does Not Foreclose* (Nashville: Abingdon Press, 1991), for a fuller understanding of this issue.
5. Barbara Schneider Fuhrmann, *Adolescence, Adolescents* (Boston: Little, Brown, 1986), p. 11.
6. For another description, see Glenn E. Ludwig, *Building an Effective Youth Ministry* (Nashville: Abingdon Press, 1979), pp. 53-54.
7. For further exploration of this topic, see Charles Webb Courtoy, "A Historical Analysis of the Three Eras of Mainline Protestant Youth Work in America as a Basis for Clues for the Future of Youth Work" (D.Min. diss., Vanderbilt University, 1976).
8. Another way of thinking about this concept comes from a diagram from the book *The Teaching Church: Moving Christian Education to Center Stage* (Nashville: Abingdon Press, 1993). Notice how different churches have different aspects of what we are calling youth ministry. Not every church has a youth fellowship.

2. Images for Youth Ministry

1. Michael Warren, "A Theory of Images in Cultural Systems: Towards Religious Cultural Contestation," Unpublished paper, Association of Professors and Researchers in Religious Education, 1989.

2. Indeed, many educators are noticing the same thing about students. They find that students are less and less able to analyze an argument in logical categories; instead they state the argument's thesis and then seek a graphic illustration to either support it or rebut it. See ibid.

3. I first heard this phrase used by David Ng, currently teaching courses in Christian education at San Francisco Theological Seminary.

4. William Myers has referred to this image as the "Lone Ranger" model. See his article, "Church in the World: Models of Youth Ministry," *Theology Today* (April 1987): 102-110. You may prefer the "Lone Ranger" image that Myers refers to, where the Lone Ranger and his faithful few adults—Tontos—shoot their "silver bullets" of programs, ministering to the adolescents who have been attracted by the Lone Ranger or Merlin.

5. Helen Keller, *The Story of My Life* (Garden City, N.Y.: Doubleday, 1904), pp. 23-24.

6. See Malcolm L. Warford, "Metanoia: A Way of Thinking About Christian Education," *New Conversations* 2, 2 (Fall 1977): 7.

7. Dean E. Feldmeyer, "Building a 'Storm Home' for Youth Ministry," *The Christian Ministry* (July 1987): 7.

8. William Myers, *Black and White Styles of Youth Ministry: Two Congregations in America* (Cleveland: Pilgrim Press, 1990).

9. Don Webb enabled worship to come alive for me in several ways. First, he helped us as youth participate in planning and executing worship. This taught us about worship and helped us appreciate what we as a faith community were about. Second, the liturgy (especially music and written responses) and the preached word related to the world that we youth lived in every day. In other words, he made the gospel relevant to us. And third, his personal style was one of approachability. He did not work directly with the youth group or Sunday school, but we youth knew we could talk to him—and often did.

10. Michael Warren, *Youth, Gospel, Liberation* (San Francisco: Harper & Row, 1987), pp. 67-68.

11. Originally I referred to this image as the "ugly duckling" image, in that we need to see the beautiful swans in the "ugly ducklings" of youth in the church and in the world. Upon further reflection, my sense is that those who see the swan in youth never see an "ugly

duckling." Rather, they have a special kind of vision, as Warren says, the eye of the artist or lover. Thus we need to approach youth ministry as an artist approaches a canvas, already imagining the beautiful work. Perhaps, the Markan account of the parable of the sower can be helpful at this point. The account in the Gospel of Mark, it would appear, emphasizes the idea that God's grace flourishes in unlikely places—even in youth.

12. Jeff Johnson, *Evangelization of Youth: An Incarnational Approach*, an Occasional Paper #1 (Nantucket, Conn.: The Center for Youth Ministry Development, 1986), p. 12.

3. Key Ingredients for Effective and Faithful Youth Ministry

1. Roland Martinson recognizes this fact by titling his book *Effective Youth Ministry* (Minneapolis: Augsburg, 1988).

2. Dean R. Hoge et al., "Desired Outcomes of Religious Education and Youth Ministry in Six Denominations," in *Religious Education Ministry with Youth*, eds. D. Campbell Wyckoff and Don Richter (Birmingham, Ala.: Religious Education Press, 1982), pp. 136-37.

3. See Duffy Robbins, *The Ministry of Nurture* (Grand Rapids: Zondervan, 1990), p. 17.

4. Michael Warren, *Giving Direction to Youth Ministry*, five audiocassettes. National Catholic Reporter Publishing Company, Kansas City, Mo., 1985.

5. Frederick Buechner, *Telling the Truth: The Gospel as Tragedy, Comedy and Fairy Tale* (New York: Harper & Row, 1977), pp. 7-8.

6. Beth Richardson, *Alive Now*, September/October 1985.

7. Search Institute, *Summary of Findings Young Adolescents and Their Parents* (Minneapolis: Search Institute, 1984).

8. Grant Shockley, "Ethnicity in Religious Education," Miller-Fondren Lecture, Scarritt College, April 1985.

9. Basil Karp, "The World View in American Government Textbooks," *Education for the World View*, Christian Education: Shared Approaches curriculum.

10. John L. Parker, Jr., *Once a Runner* (Cedar Mountain, N.C.: Cedar Winds Publishing, 1978), p. 12.

4. Building Strong Relationships

1. See Charles R. Foster and Grant S. Shockley, eds., *Working with Black Youth* (Nashville: Abingdon Press, 1989) and Gwendolyn Rice, "Young Black Men, the Church, and Our Future," *Chicago Theological Seminary Register* 78 (Spring 1988): 10-15.

5. The Right Adults

1. *Maturity*, as I'm using the word, does not necessarily mean chronological age, although a mature faith is most usually associated with an older person than with a young one. For more on Christian maturity, see Peter L. Benson and Carolyn H. Eklin, *Effective Christian Education: A National Study of Protestant Congregations* (Minneapolis: Search Institute, 1990).

2. Larry Kefauver, *Starting a Youth Ministry* (Loveland, Col.: Group Books, 1984), p. 13.

3. "Four Phases of Ease" can be found in J. David Stone, ed., *The Complete Youth Ministries Handbook*, vol. 1 (Nashville: Abingdon Press, 1979), in the chapter "Youth Ministry Today: Overview and Concepts."

4. A number of excellent books cover the topic of supporting volunteers. I would recommend these four as a place to start: Alvin Lindgren and Norman Shawchuck, *Let My People Go: Empowering Laity for Ministry* (Nashville: Abingdon Press, 1980); Les Christie, *Unsung Heroes: How to Recruit and Train Volunteer Youth Workers* (Grand Rapids: Zondervan, 1987); Douglas W. Johnson, *The Care and Feeding of Volunteers* (Nashville: Abingdon Press, 1978); J. David Stone and Rose Mary Miller, *Volunteer Youth Workers* (Loveland, Col.: Group Books, 1985).

6. Choosing Topics and Developing Youth Ministry Programming

1. See Erik Erikson, *Identity: Youth and Crisis* (New York: Norton, 1968); *Childhood and Society* (New York: Norton, 1986); James Fowler, *Stages of Faith: The Psychology of Human Development and the Quest for Meaning* (San Francisco: Harper & Row, 1981); Joan Lipsitz, *Growing Up Forgotten* (Lexington, Mass.: Lexington Books, 1977); David Elkind, *All Grown Up and No Place to Go: Teenagers in Crisis* (Reading, Mass.: Addison-Wesley, 1984); and *The Hurried Child: Growing Up Too Fast, Too Soon* (Reading, Mass.: Addison-Wesley, 1988); Joseph Kett, *Rites of Passage: Adolescence in America* (New York: Basic Books, 1977); Lawrence Kohlberg and Thomas Lockona, *The Stages of Ethical Development* (San Francisco: Harper & Row, 1986).

2. See Reinhold Niebuhr, *The Nature and Destiny of Man* (New York: Charles Scribner and Sons, 1943).

3. This work has not addressed the problem of culture and Christ. How one as a Christian is going to relate to the culture in which one lives and works has been an ongoing issue for Christians since Jesus' day. H. Richard Niebuhr's classic work *Christ and Culture* (New York:

Harper and Bros., 1951) is still the most helpful, in my opinion, at examining this issue. Youth ministry has always been concerned with this issue. For example, the earliest youth groups, The Christian Endeavor Societies, struggled with whether to have dances in the 1880s.

4. See Frank Ferrell and Janet Ferrell, with Edward Wakin, *Trevor's Place: The Story of the Boy Who Brings Hope to the Homeless* (New York: Harper & Row, 1985).

7. Resources for Program

1. See Matthew Fox, *Original Blessing* (Sante Fe, N.M.: Bear and Company, 1983).

8. Working with Other Youth Ministry Organizations

1. Barbara Schneider Fuhrmann, *Adolescence, Adolescents* (Boston: Little, Brown, 1986), p. 432.
2. Ibid., p. 457.
3. Interestingly, the Scouting movement is no longer located in the area of Christian education or youth ministry in The United Methodist Church but is under the auspices of United Methodist Men. In 1956 the UM Men were directed by the *Discipline* to cooperate with Scouting or 4-H Clubs or similar organizations. But it wasn't until recent staff cuts and budget problems in the Board of Discipleship, under which the Christian Education Section is located, that the Scouting movement was officially moved to the United Methodist Men. Currently The United Methodist Church funds a denominational position that relates to the Scouting movement at the national level. There has been talk of starting an endowment campaign to fully fund this position outside of denominational finances.
4. Information in this section was gathered from four main sources: personal interviews; personal and professional contact; "Footprints Focus" in *Footprints* 7, 3 (Spring 1984); and Judy Fletcher, "Much Ado About Something," 1976.
5. Information gathered from *Fateful Choices*, by Fred M. Hechinger, Carnegie Corporation, 1992; *A Matter of Time: Risk and Opportunity in the Nonschool Hours*, The Report of the Task Force on Youth Development and Community programs, Carnegie Corporation, 1992; *Directory of Youth Leadership Groups*, Linda L. Little and Richard E. Steele, Mershon Center, Ohio State University, 1990.

9. A Youth Fellowship Model

1. The idea being put forth stands in the tradition of Paulo Freire, *Pedagogy of the Oppressed* (New York: Seabury, 1970); and Tom Groome, *Christian Religious Education* (San Francisco: Harper & Row, 1980), when they discuss action/reflection education.
2. See Peter Benson and Eugene Roehlkepartain, *Beyond Leaf Raking: Learning to Serve/Serving to Learn* (Nashville: Abingdon Press, 1993).
3. Soren Kierkegaard, *Purity of the Heart Is to Will One Thing* (New York: Harper and Bros., 1948), pp. 180-81.
4. See William Myers, *Black and White Styles of Youth Ministry* (New York: Pilgrim Press, 1991); Betty Jane and J. Martin Bailey, *Youth Plan Worship* (Pilgrim Press, 1987); Jerry O. Cook, *Worship Resources for Youth* (Champaign, Ill.: C-4 Resources, 1983); Dennis Benson, *Creative Worship in Youth Ministry* (Loveland, Col.: Group, 1985).

10. Making Youth Fellowship Work

1. In most cases the planning process is not something I want to bog down the entire group doing, especially if the youth fellowship has a number of community and show-up level youth in attendance. Nothing can be more deadly than sitting through a poorly run planning process about which you have little knowledge or investment.

LINCOLN CHRISTIAN COLLEGE AND SEMINARY